When FOOTBALL *Was* FOOTBALL

NORWICH CITY

First published in 2012

A catalogue record for this book is available from the British Library

ISBN: 978-0-857331-70-0

Published by Haynes Publishing, Sparkford, Yeovil,
Somerset BA22 7JJ, UK
Tel: 01963 442030 Fax: 01963 440001
Int. tel: +44 1963 442030 Int. fax: +44 1963 440001
E-mail: sales@haynes.co.uk
Website: www.haynes.co.uk

Haynes North America Inc., 861 Lawrence Drive,
Newbury Park, California 91320, USA

Creative Director: Kevin Gardner
Designed for Haynes by BrainWave

Printed and bound in the US

When FOOTBALL *Was* FOOTBALL

NORWICH CITY

A Nostalgic Look at a Century of the Club

Iain Dale

Contents

Foreword

The fact that you have bought this book shows that you, like me, have a love for Norwich City Football Club, its history and its personalities. It is a unique club, one that inspires tremendous loyalty both from its fans and players. And that's why this book is so important. It introduces the glorious history of this great club to a new generation of fans.

When I signed for Norwich City on a work experience scheme in 1983, one of the first things that I had drilled into me was that I would be expected to play football the "Norwich City way".

Footballing men like Ken Brown, Mel Machin, Dave Stringer and Ronnie Brooks would emphasize that Norwich City was a club that played football the right way: for the keeper to throw the ball out, to steadily build the move, pass the ball below knee height, work it to the strikers, pass and move, pass and move – good to watch, of course, and very effective.

I have subscribed to that football belief ever since. Growing up at the club I watched some great players demonstrate this way of playing the game, people like Steve Bruce and Dave Watson. Yes, they were central defenders, but they could play the game, preferring the ball at their feet, not in the air. Likewise Mick McGuire, Mark Barham, Mick Channon and Chris Woods; also John Deehan, not only a natural goalscorer, but a clever footballer who could adapt and play in just about any position. Later on there was Ian Crook, with whom I was fortunate to share the Norwich midfield. He was a player blessed with footballing genius and as good as any midfielder in British football at that time.

We were coached to play football this way right throughout the club, from us fresh faced "kids" right through to the first teamers. We must have been doing something right because, in my first season we won the FA Youth Cup – the first, and, to date, the only time Norwich City have achieved that honour. It took three matches to see off Everton in the final, but our belief in ourselves and the way we wanted to play the game saw us through. I scored in the Carrow Road game and what a thrill that was, giving me a hunger to only ever play for Norwich City and to win more trophies, winning by playing great football, and playing alongside other great players.

I loved playing for Norwich and was determined to succeed. And I'd been at Carrow Road for nearly a decade when Mike Walker embedded me into his side when he became manager. He was another man that wanted to play the game in the right manner, and again we proved that it could work, finishing third in the Premiership in 1993 and qualifying to play in the UEFA Cup – another first for Norwich City during my time at the club. The team that beat Bayern Munich and the memory of that goal I scored will stay with me forever.

It helped, of course, that we had fans who appreciated what we were trying to do – magnificent fans, noisy, passionate, committed to their club, the city and the great county of Norfolk. They genuinely are a 12th man. Norwich City are a community club, with fans every bit as important as anyone or anything else at Carrow Road.

With this book, Iain has looked back at the history of Norwich City and celebrated all that is extraordinary about the club – players, managers, matches, successes and failures, and, of course, the fans. Norwich is an iconic club with a rich history, as the following pages prove. It's a proper football club that has always tried to do things the right way – as I soon learnt!

A special club that deserves this special book. Enjoy it.

Jeremy Goss

Introduction

Norwich City Football Club. Four words that have come to mean so much to so many over the years. It's a club that is loved by hundreds of thousands of fans across Norfolk, but its appeal stretches way beyond the boundaries of God's own county. If you exclude the people who inexplicably support that club in East Suffolk, Norwich City is a club which is both liked and respected by most football fans all over the country. They associate Norwich with a brand of football that has stayed true to the sport's roots, which is both entertaining and attractive. There is a certain Norwich style. You know it when you see it. It's been exemplified by a string of top-class players down the years.

Everyone knows Norwich City as the Canaries. It's one of the most famous nicknames in football. The Canaries have been part of my life ever since I was a child growing up in north Essex. Ipswich may have been nearer, but Norwich was always seen by my family as the capital of East Anglia. It didn't stop me growing up as a West Ham fan – I was easily led as a child – but there was always something special about Norwich. My Auntie Jean, an inspiration from my childhood, would drive up to Norwich every other Saturday, ostensibly to go to a Canaries game, although we always speculated she was seeing her fancy man.

In 1981 I started my degree course at the University of East Anglia. And it was then that I became a regular at Carrow Road. Norwich had just been relegated to Division Two so I was denied the opportunity of seeing them play West Ham that season. However, I was a regular at home games throughout the 1980s and saw some great players – Chris Woods, Dave Watson and Steve Bruce. Brucey was my favourite player of the time – a no-nonsense player who was far more skilful than he was ever given credit for. Gillingham, his first club, are another one of my teams and I remember him breaking his left leg three yards in front of me. The crunch had to be heard to be believed.

This book is a unique collection of memorable and evocative photographs dating from the birth of the club right through to its first season in the newly formed Premier League in 1992. Most of the photos are taken from the *Daily Mirror* and *Eastern Daily Press* archives and many are previously unpublished. From the early days of the club at the Nest, through to their election to the Football League in 1920, the cup glory of 1959, the thrills of promotions and the heartache of relegations, and then eventually promotion to the big time in 1972, this book will evoke memories for older fans and introduce younger fans to the club's proud history. The book culminates in telling the story of cup glory in the 1970s and 1980s and ends with the 1993–94 UEFA cup run. It's designed to take you through the entire history of one of Britain's most entertaining football clubs and bring to life many of the events, games and characters some newer fans may not have previously come across. Legends such as Ron Ashman, Kevin Keelan and Duncan Forbes are all pictured, along with scenes from many of the Canaries' most memorable games through the decades.

I hope that after reading this book you will have a greater understanding of the history of this great club and what makes it tick. This is the story of Norwich City Football Club. On the Ball, City!

Iain Dale

Three Canaries legends: Kevin Keelan, Duncan Forbes and Dave Stringer.

From Citizens to Canaries
1902-1920

The Nest, home of Norwich City FC from 1908 until the move to Carrow Road in 1935.

The Founding of a Football Club

Norwich City Football Club was incorporated on 17th June 1902 by club founders Robert Webster and Joseph Cowper Nutchey. Three days earlier a notice had appeared in the *Eastern Daily Press* that a meeting would be held at the Criterion Café in White Lion Street, in the centre of Norwich. It proved to be a success and those present were enthusiastic about the prospect of encouraging a higher level of football in the city. It was immediately decided to base the club at the Newmarket Road ground, which ended up being the club's home for its first six years, before a move to the Nest in Rosary Road on the north side of the city. Newmarket Road was already being used for local football matches by Norfolk County FA and local schools. It was the only ground in the city which had a grandstand, albeit one that could hold fewer than 500 spectators. A rent of £25 per annum was agreed.

The first match, played at Newmarket Road, took place on 6th September 1902, in front of a respectable crowd of just over 2,000 fans. The friendly, against Harwich & Parkeston was a reasonable test for the new club, who had recruited players throughout the summer from a number of local Norfolk teams.

Club president and future Foreign Secretary Sir Samuel Hoare kicked off the game, which ended in a 1-1 draw. Jimmy Shields will forever be remembered as the first man to score a goal for Norwich City. As a sign of how far the club was to progress in its first three years, when the teams met again in another friendly in 1905, Norwich ran out 11-1 winners.

FOOTBALL.

JOHN BOWMAN SPEAKS OUT

ONLY STEADY MEN WANTED

A BEDINGFIELD STORY.

Mr. John William Bowman, the player
manager who is to shape the destinies of the
Norwich City F.C., Ltd., and pilot them through
the thorny paths of professionalism, arrived at
Norwich yesterday by the 1.18 train from Liverpool Street. The late manager of the Queen's
Park Rangers was met at Norwich Thorpe Station by Messrs. Wilfrid L. Burgess (chairman),
C. C. Fielding (secretary), and P. F. Robertson
(director), and proceeded to the Criterion Cafe.
We were permitted to intrude upon the privacy
of the little luncheon party, and a few minutes
of conversation revealed to us the secret of Bowman's popularity. Frankness seems stamped
upon his agreeable features, and the expected
touch of vanity, suggested by the trimly cut and
pointed moustaches, vanishes as the new
manager talks easily and pleasantly, and with
just the suspicion of an accent of a Midlander.
Not every man glows with enthusiasm when the
topic of conversation turns upon his daily work,
but as the light kindles in John Bowman's
bright grey eyes, it is easy to see that he loves
the game and the sport none the less because it
happens to be the medium of his weekly wage.
One feels instinctively that Bowman has all
that is best in the professional character; his
forehead, from which the dark hair is brushed
upwards, seems to indicate the brainy, intelligent player who makes for the good of the game.

LEFT: City manager and director, Arthur Turner.

ABOVE: Norwich City's first professional manager, John Bowman.

LEFT: *Eastern Daily Press* report on John Bowman.

ABOVE: Norwich City team photo, 1905–06.

Norwich Team: William "Dillo" Sparks, George Bardwell, William Cracknell, Walter Crome, Geno Yallop, Jack Yallop, Fred Witham, Bertie Playford, Robert Collinson (captain), Jimmy Shields and Tommy Newell.

The club's first captain was Robert Collinson, a Yorkshireman who had played county cricket for Yorkshire. He also represented Norfolk at athletics. He was the first Norwich City player to score a penalty and was the first scorer of a hat-trick.

'On the Ball, City!'

Tommy Newell leads Norwich out in the amateur days at Newmarket Road.

ABOVE: James Peacock in 1911, an outside-left who played for Norwich four times in the first team.

ABOVE: Reg Levi signed up to Norwich City on the 30th August 1910 alongside his brother Harold. They were one of the earliest sets of brothers to sign for City.

ON THE BALL, CITY!

In the days to call, which we have left behind,
Our boyhood's glorious game,
And our youthful vigour has declined
With its mirth and its lonesome end;
You will think of the time, the happy time,
Its memories fond recall
When in the bloom of our youthful prime
We've kept upon the ball.

Kick off, throw it in, have a little scrimmage,
Keep it low, a splendid rush, bravo, win or die;
On the ball, City, never mind the danger
Steady on, now's your chance,
Hurrah! We've scored a goal.

Let all tonight then drink with me
To the football game we love,
And wish it may successful be
As other games of old,
And in one grand united toast
Join player, game and song,
And fondly pledge your pride and toast,
Success to the City club.

Kick off, throw it in, have a little scrimmage,
Keep it low, a splendid rush, bravo, win or die;
On the ball, City, never mind the danger,
Steady on, now's your chance,
Hurrah! We've scored a goal.

Words by Arthur T Smith, a director of the club 1905–07.

It is thought that the song 'On the Ball, City' was actually written in the 1890s for either the Norwich Teachers or Caley's FC. The original version included the line "On the ball, Teachers, Never mind your features."

LEFT: Fred "Sonny" Wilkinson made his debut for City as a right-half in 1910, and went on to make a further 68 appearances.

The Strip

During the first six years of the club's existence, they were given the nickname of the Citizens. It was only when they moved to the Nest in 1908 that the club were officially nicknamed the Canaries, although the name had been used before then. During this period the club's shirts were very different to those of today. They wore light blue-and-white shirts, with the right-hand half being blue and the left-hand white. It was only at the start of the 1907–08 season, the year before the ground move that the players first wore yellow shirts. They also wore white shorts and black stockings. It is thought that during that first season the original plain yellow shirts were replaced by ones with a small canary logo on the left-hand breast and a laced collar. The blue-and-white shirts were still worn occasionally; while the concept of an "away" strip wasn't around then, there were occasions when the yellow strip clashed with that of the opposing team.

The evolution of the kit.

1905–07	Blue-and-white halves
1907–09	Yellow, green collar and sleeves
1909–23	Yellow and green
1923–27	White with a canary badge
1927–47	Yellow-and-green halves
1947–65	Variations of yellow shirt, black shorts
1965–70	Yellow shirt, black or green shorts
1970 onwards	Yellow shirt, green shorts

The Road to Professionalism

> *I had to enlist the services of about 50 players, and as they were all amateurs you can understand how great my task was. Luckily for me I was well known.*
>
> Arthur Turner

ABOVE: This is one of the few surviving pictures of Norwich City's early days. It is from the Southern League game at Portsmouth on 14th September 1907. Here you can see City goalkeeper Fred Thompson punching away a Portsmouth attack.

Only three weeks after their formation the club were elected to the Norfolk & Suffolk League but their first competitive match played at Newmarket Road was an FA Amateur Cup tie on 11th October 1902. The opponents were Lynn Town, who were walloped 5-0.

The first visit of Norfolk & Suffolk League opponents Ipswich Town came on 15th November, with Norwich running out 1-0 winners. In the return fixture on 13th December Norwich completed the double with a 2-1 win over the team who would become their fiercest rivals. In their first two seasons in the league, Norwich finished in a respectable third place.

As the 1903–04 season beckoned, manager Arthur Turner made a real effort to attract new talent to Newmarket Road. He poached three star players from Norfolk & Suffolk League champions, Lowestoft Town – Langford Baker, Percy Gooch and Edmund Chamberlin – and signed ageing goalkeeper Bill Cooks from Kirkley, along with Horace "Moosh" King and Bob Pointer from local village team, Catton.

Turner was the lynchpin of the club during its formative years. Former captain of Thorpe Hamlet and secretary of Norwich Swifans he knew how to organize and was a real sporting all-rounder. It was he who had recruited around 50 players to form four teams who played under the Norwich City banner. Apart from Newmarket Road, the club's reserve teams also played at Delf's Meadow in City Road and at Dix's Land.

The 1904–05 season saw more new signings, the most notable of which was Herbert Vigar from Redhill, who proceeded to score 12 goals in 14 games in his first season with the Citizens. Norwich won their first five games, but dark clouds were appearing on the horizon in the form of an FA inquiry into the club's affairs.

For the first three years of their life, Norwich City existed as an amateur side, but in late 1904 allegations were made that the club had been making illicit payments to their players and using money to induce players from other clubs to sign for them. The Football Association decided to investigate and found them guilty. The club quickly agreed to accept the findings, but rather than accept a fine, they decided to turn the club into a proper professional outfit. But there were internal consequences. The two founding fathers of the club, Joseph Nutchey and Robert Webster, were both suspended, as was their fellow director, Arthur Turner. Robert Collinson took over as chairman and was successful in persuading the Norfolk & Suffolk League not to expel them; they completed the season and finished as champions, winning the club's first piece of silverware. The club were on the up.

The three suspended directors were quickly reinstated and the club appointed their first full-time manager, headhunting John Bowman from Queens Park Rangers.

"Without the knowledge of my fellow officers, I set to work and secured several players who, I knew, would greatly strengthen our team. Four of them I secured from Lowestoft Town. Naturally, I had to find jobs in Norwich for them, and this was a bit of a problem. But after much work and worry I was successful. I still kept this a secret, till one evening one of our local papers issued a fly-sheet the whole of which was taken by the announcement, 'Lowestoft Players for Norwich City'. In the paper itself a whole column was devoted to the news, which caused a big sensation. My fellow officers lost no time in coming to see me to find out if what they had read was really true. I had to assure them that it was. My reason for keeping the news to myself was that I did not want it to leak out as efforts might have been made to induce the players to return to Lowestoft before they settled in Norwich. I always liked to work alone."

Arthur Turner on his player signings before the 1903–04 season

"In a weak moment, I was induced to take over the chairmanship of Norwich City Football Club after some venerable and kindly gentlemen had held an inquiry into our amateur status and suspended all our best trusted officials. We took the plunge into professionalism, essayed to form a limited company with £5,000 capital and boldly, perhaps cheekily, applied for admission to the Southern League. The great difficulty at first was to persuade the delegates that there was a place called Norwich. There was only one thing to do – bring them to Norwich, which we did in a special saloon from Liverpool Street."

Wilfred Burgess

Wilfred L Burgess, the first chairman of the professional club, which was formed on 4th March 1905.

BELOW: More action from the 1907 game v Portsmouth. Portsmouth's James Thompson is pictured scoring a penalty at Fratton Park. The game finished in a 1-1 draw. The Norwich team that day were: Thompson, Newlands, McEwen, Hutchinson, Bushell, Livingstone, Muir, Young, Bauchop, Smith, Allsopp.

BELOW LEFT: J Byrne, 1906–07. BELOW RIGHT: P McLarney, 1906–07.

–LEGENDS–

Davie Ross

Long before the outcry over the departures of legends Kevin Reeves, Ron Davies and Hugh Curran, there was Davie Ross. He signed for Norwich in 1905, and scored 49 times in just 71 appearances. So when it was decided to transfer him to Manchester City in 1907 for a Southern League record fee of £650 there was considerable outrage by fans. Ross was an inaugural member of the Norwich City FC Hall of Fame.

"There was outcry when City sold [their] star forward… to Manchester City in February 1907 for a Southern League record fee of £650, plus a guaranteed £250 from a friendly – a sign of things to come for a club who have so often sold their star goalscorers."

Norwich Evening News on the transfer of Davie Ross

BELOW: Davie Ross in 1906, one of the earliest pictures of a Norwich City player.

FOOTBALL –STATS–

Davie Ross

Name: Davie Ross
Born: 8th January 1883
Died: 2nd January 1947
Position: Inside-left
Norwich City Playing Career: 1905–07
Club Appearances: 71
Goals: 49

FA Cup Glory

In 1905–06, only three years after their formation, Norwich City moved up to what at the time must have seemed the big time. Their application to join the Southern League was accepted on 30th May 1905. The professional era had started. But it was a close run thing. The Southern League was a very serious competition in those days (Southern League members Tottenham Hotspur had won the 1901 FA Cup) and many were sceptical about Norwich City's application. Norfolk might as well have been Mars, as far as some of the league's administrators were concerned. A hearts and minds campaign was embarked upon by the club with Southern League honchos being wined and dined and shown the club's facilities. Only two places were available and Norwich were competing against Crystal Palace, Luton Town, Clapton Orient and Leyton & Grays United. In the end it was Luton

"As soon as we were old enough to go to the Nest on our own, my twin brother and I established a regular watching-place on the top of what we called the 'Spion Cop'. Here, we were at the top of a sheer concrete wall, some twenty or thirty feet high. It bounded the playing area within a yard of the touchline at the Thorpe End of the ground. The wall was a terrifying object to any outside left who faced it, but we had a splendid view from the top. It was here that Jimmy Stoakes, as fast and as brave an outside left as ever played for City, broke his leg as he crashed into the concrete. The crack resounded all over the ground."

Ted Bell

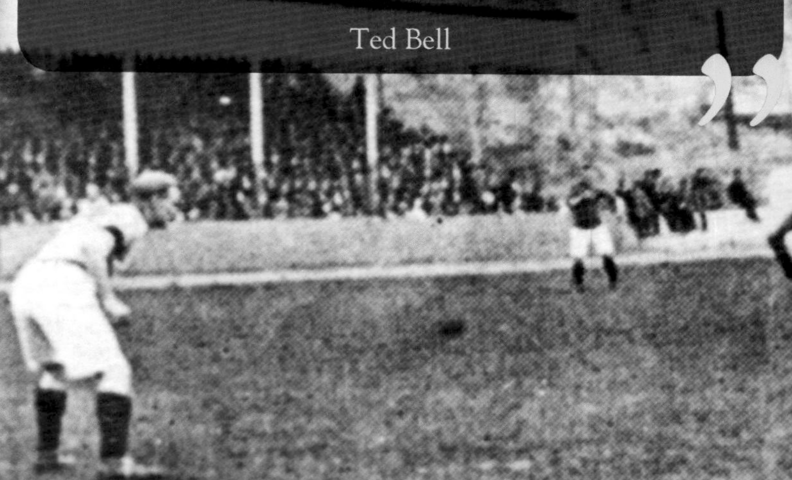

and Norwich who triumphed.

Bowman signed new players and, on 2nd September 1905, Norwich City's 11-season stint in the Southern League commenced with a 2-0 away defeat to Plymouth Argyle. A week later in the first home league game, the Citizens drew 1-1 with Southampton. Despite this inauspicious start, the team did well in its first season and finished seventh.

During the season the club sought to raise £1,500 in new funds to expand the club. Two leading Norwich businessmen joined the board and it seemed all was well. The club balance sheet showed a loss of just over £500 but there seemed no reason to worry. But midway through the 1906–07 season the cracks started to show. In order to raise funds the board decided to sell top scorer Davie Ross (by this time he had already scored 28 goals) to Manchester City for £650. The fans were outraged and staged demonstrations, but these were to no avail. The crisis resulted in the resignation of board members and, on 19th June, manager John Bowman also left the club.

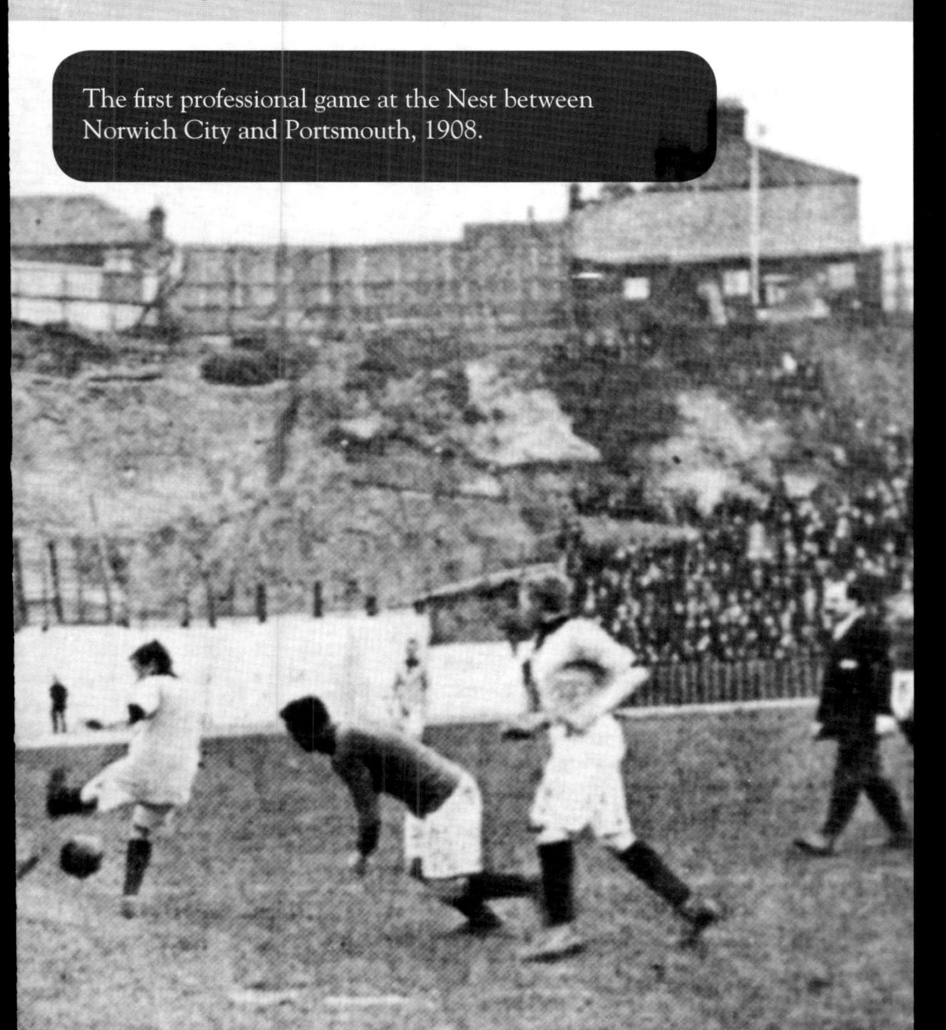

The first professional game at the Nest between Norwich City and Portsmouth, 1908.

Norwich City's first outing in the FA Cup came in the 1902–03 season with a 5-0 away derby defeat against Lowestoft Town in the preliminary round. It wasn't until 1905–06 that Norwich reached the first round proper, when they beat Tunbridge Wells Rangers 5-0 in a replay after a 1-1 home draw. But the run was short-lived and Norwich were well and truly beaten by Manchester United 3-0 in the second round. In 1908–09 Norwich reached the third round for the first time, this time going out to Bristol City. Earlier in the competition, a first-round replay had had to be played on a neutral ground, Stamford Bridge, after Reading alleged that the Nest pitch was not of a standard size. Justice prevailed and Norwich triumphed 3-2.

In their six years at Newmarket Road, Norwich's biggest game came on 11th January 1908, when the Citizens played the FA Cup holders, Division One giants, The Wednesday, in a FA Cup first-round tie. More than 10,300 spectators crammed into the ground, having paid between one and four shillings for tickets (between 5p and 20p in today's money) to witness a famous 2-0 victory by the Southern League minnows.

This match provided the impetus to the club's directors to move to a bigger ground, a move which proved very necessary when the Newmarket Road landlords decided to increase the rent and impose new restrictions on the ground's use. Four thousand spectators watched the last game played at Newmarket Road, which took place on 25th April 1908 – a 3-1 win against Swindon Town. The highest attendance at Newmarket Road was 11,500; they watched Norwich City beat Tottenham Hotspur 4-1 on 14th April 1906.

Today, the Newmarket Road ground is still used as playing fields and is located just off the Norwich ring road near the A11 junction and Notcutts Garden Centre.

"Although there were many difficulties at Norwich and much to put up with, our friendship was to me one of the bright spots in a clouded sky… You carried out some delicate tasks with great tact and no small amount of the success we achieved was due to your efforts."

Letter from John Bowman to Arthur Turner, written several years after he left the club

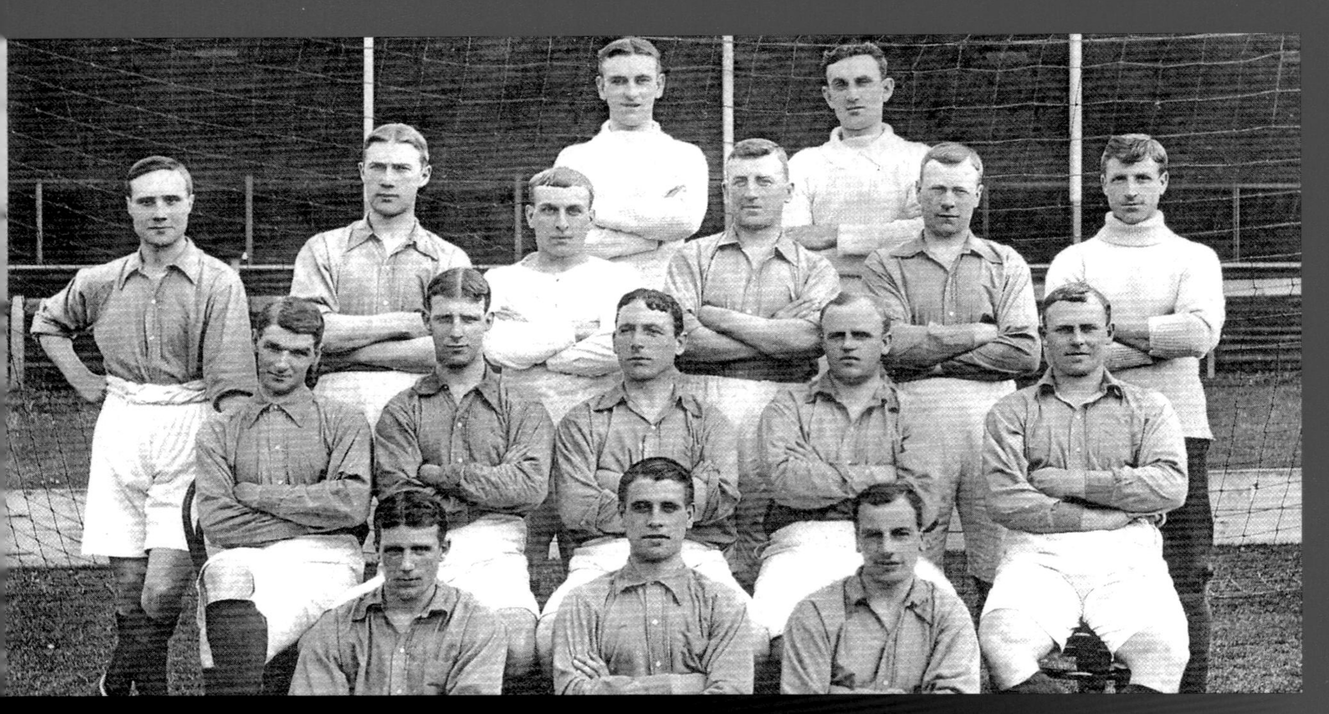

LEFT: 1907–08 team at Newmarket Road, shortly before moving to the Nest. Back row (left to right): Peter Roney, Fred Thompson. Third row: Billy Bushell, Albert Jones, Bobby Whiteman, Archie Livingstone, Gerry Newlands, Hugh McQueen (assistant trainer). Second row: Robert Muir, George Lamberton, James McEwen, Wally Smith, Tommy Allsopp. Front row: James Young, Jimmy Bauchop, Harry Hutchinson.

The United League

ABOVE: Norwich City manager, Jimmy "Punch" McEwen.

In only their second year of professional football, Norwich City also entered the United League at the start of the 1906–07 season. This was a midweek league with matches being played on Monday, Wednesday or Thursday afternoons. It was contested by eight clubs including Brighton & Hove Albion, Luton Town, Watford and Crystal Palace. In their first game, the Citizens won 4-2 away at Leyton, with Willie Wood scoring twice. At the end of the season Norwich finished fourth, having won six of the 14 games.

The following season Norwich did not enter the competition. Boardroom fights and the lack of a manager were the probable reasons, but in 1908–09 they entered the United League for the second time and played matches at the Nest. By this time the league had become one predominantly centred on Midlands-based clubs. It became very expensive for Norwich to travel to away games and as the season went on, more and more fringe players were being selected. A decision was taken not to continue with membership of the United League and their last match in the league proved to be a 7-0 away victory at Grantham, with Sam Gunton signing off with a five-goal haul. In the event, City finished in third place, only a point behind champions Rotherham.

It was on 5th September 1908, in a Southern League fixture, that Norwich suffered what remains their heaviest defeat – 10-2 away to Swindon Town. Ernie Coxhead and Willie Silor were the Norwich scorers and the team was already 6-1 down at half-time. Perhaps it was a reaction to the move earlier in the summer from Newmarket Road to the Nest, which was to remain the club's home until 1935. Norwich had played at Luton on the 2nd September and bizarrely the previous day had met Fulham in a friendly at the Nest in order to christen it. Three games in five days proved to be too much, especially for a team without a manager: Jimmy McEwen's services had been dispensed with at the end of the 1907–08 season. No new appointment was made and it fell to a combination of the club's directors and Arthur Turner to manage the side.

The following Saturday was a momentous one for the fledgling Canaries. They played their first competitive match at their new home, the Nest. Having moved from the south side of the city centre to the north, it was a match keenly anticipated by the club's supporters. Portsmouth were the visitors. City fans must have expected the worst, having shipped 14 goals in their previous two league games, and having Jimmy McEwen carried off with a career-ending injury after only half an hour, but to everyone's surprise the game ended goalless.

The 1908–09 season brought with it an elongated first-round tie against Reading, which saw Norwich eventually triumph in a second replay by a 3-2 margin. In the next round Norwich had what looked like an unwinnable draw away against Liverpool at Anfield. It was anything but, and Norwich again won in the last minute through a goal from John Smith.

Unfortunately the cup run was ended in the next round by Bristol City and the season went downhill from there, with City finishing third from bottom in the league. Perhaps they weren't helped by giving three games to a player listed each time in the match day programme as "A. Canary", who was described as "an old favourite who preferred to play under a no de plume".

> *The antics of the Norwich players after each goal were amusing, but were as nought compared to the scenes when the final whistle blew. The goalkeeper first turned a complete somersault, and then proceeded to embrace his two full backs. In this position they left the arena, with the goalkeeper practically suspended in mid air and the trinity locked together like three happy schoolboys.*
>
> Ted Bell

Norwich beat West Ham 2-0 on 8th October 1910 in a Southern League fixture, with goals from Freddy Wilkinson and Bill Rayner.

The 1909–10 season saw Arthur Turner remain in charge of the team, although in March 1910 his long association with the club came to an abrupt end and James Stansfield was appointed to replace him in the secretary-manager role. It was a difficult season, which saw the club just escape relegation with a 17th place finish. In April the away fixture at Southampton was played with only 10 players after the Norwich left-back Swann failed to turn up. Stansfield remained at the helm until the First World War put paid to league football. But they were inglorious times with Norwich finishing 10th, 12th, 18th, 14th and 13th. Jock Mackenzie proved to be Stansfield's best signing, with the former Carlisle full-back making 204 appearances for the club, 90 of them consecutive between 1911 and 1914. Later, the 1913–14 season saw the arrival of a real Canaries character from Portsmouth. George "Pompey" Martin played for the club until the 1926–27 season, making 337 appearances. He was so highly thought of that he was granted two testimonials.

Troubles and Resurrection

The 1913–14 team. This was the last full team before the First World War. Back row (left to right): George Bell, George MacDonald. Third row: Cecil Potter, Harry Woods, Arthur Wolstenholme, James Kennedy. Second row: Billy Hampson, Jack Houghton, Billy Ingham, Ben Smith, Joe Lansdale, William Mellor, John Allen, Frank Hill, Wally Taylor, Arthur Woodland. Front row: James B Stansfield (manager), George Martin, Percy Sutcliffe, Thomas Valentine, Charles Curtin, Alfred Boland, George Ritchie, Danny Wilson, Jock Mackenzie, Charlie Miles (trainer).

During the First World War the club experienced severe financial problems and was wound up in December 1917. A shareholders meeting was held at the Museum Café and a resolution was passed… *"That owing to the company being unable to meet its liabilities it is hereby resolved that the same be wound up voluntarily and that Mr Robert Charles Spicer of Queen Street, Norwich, incorporated accountant, be and is hereby appointed liquidator."*

More than £2,000 was owed to the bank and creditors were owed £1,000. Mr W T Blyth, who presided over the emergency meeting declared: "It is the first time I have been in the chair and it looks as if it is going to be the last."

Fellow director C T Watling, who moved the resolution, was rather more optimistic about the future. "There really is no reason why one of these days when circumstances will become more favourable, the old club should not be started again and have a glorious future."

Indeed, it was less than 18 months later that a new company was started and was accepted back into the Southern League in time to start the 1919–20 season. W T Blyth resumed his role as chairman and the club appointed Frank Buckley as manager. Norwich went out of the FA Cup 5-0 at Darlington and a few months later, in March, a new stand was opened at the Nest. And, as an aside, goalkeeper Jack Groves was suspended by the directors for insubordination. At the end of the season Norwich finished 12th.

During the season the Football League asked most of the members of the Southern League if they would be interested in forming a third division of the Football League. Norwich continued to play in the Southern League, but entered a reserve team, and twice finished as champions in the 1930s.

SOUTHERN LEAGUE RECORD

1905–06 – 7th
1906–07 – 8th
1907–08 – 16th
1908–09 – 19th
1909–10 – 17th
1910–11 – 10th
1911–12 – 12th
1912–13 – 18th
1913–14 – 14th
1914–15 – 13th
1919–20 – 12th

Overall record: P424 W135 D124 L165 F558 A610 PTS394
Most games played: Jock Mackenzie – 186
Highest goalscorer: Davie Ross – 36

These are the players who played most often for Norwich City from their formation in 1902 until their accession to the Football League in 1920. The statistics include appearances in all league and cup competitions (courtesy of Sing Up The River End).

1902–20 Players

1 Jock Mackenzie **204**
2 William Bushell **154**
3 Harold Woods **151**
4 Sam Wolstenholme **145**
5 William Hampson **141**
6= William Ingham **134**
6= Archie Livingstone **134**
8 Cecil Potter **133**
9 Tom Allsopp **132**
10 James McEwen **121**
11= Robert Beale **111**
11= Gerry Newlands **111**
13 Duncan Ronaldson **109**

The re-formed 1919–20 team after the First World War; they were managed by Major Frank Buckley but this proved to be their final season in the Southern League.

From the Nest to Carrow Road
1920-1939

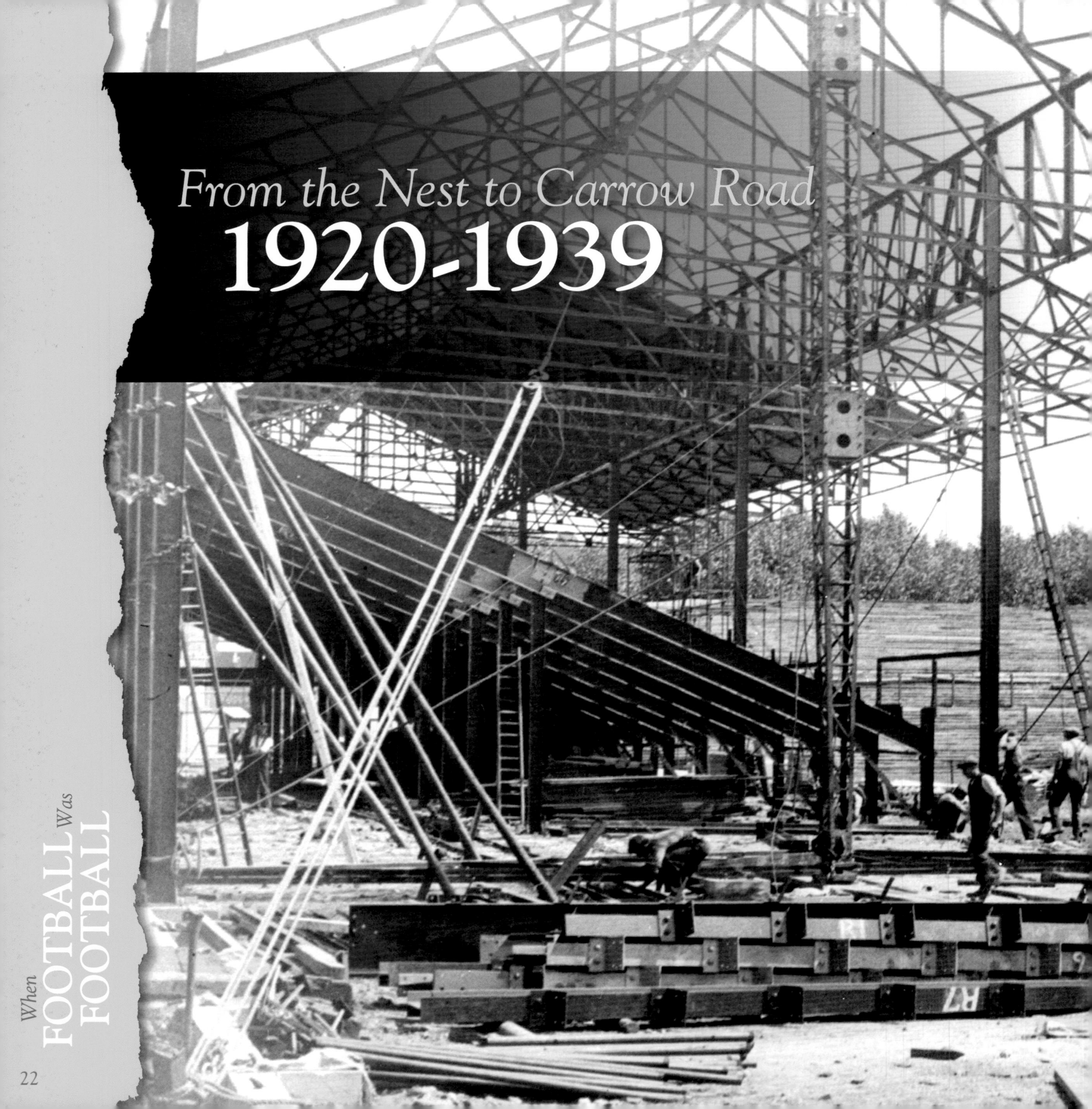

The new main stand being built at Carrow Road, summer 1935.

Oldest Players

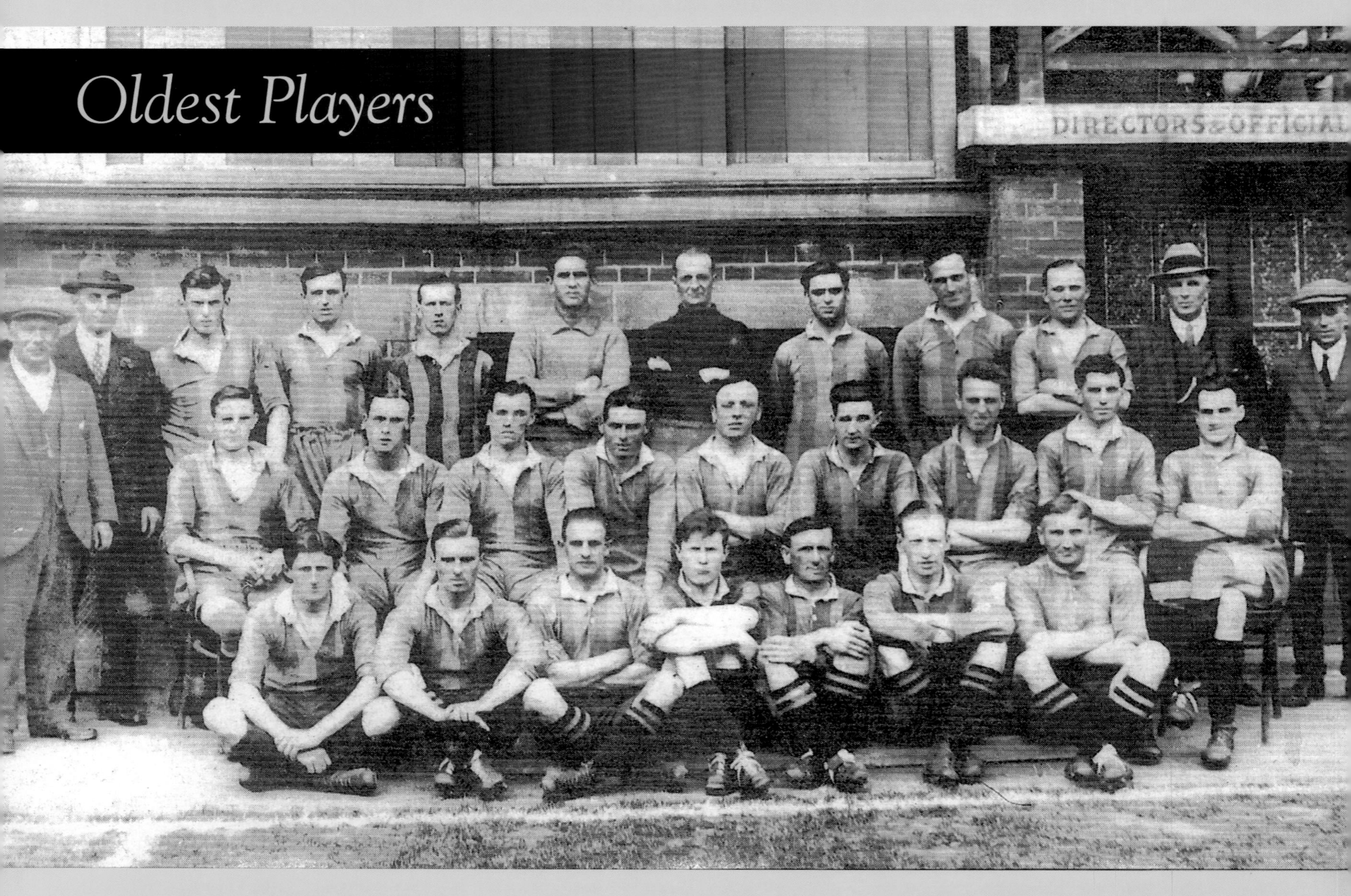

ABOVE: The 1922–23 team. Goalkeeper Charles Dennington can be seen sixth from the left on the back row; he was the first goalkeeper to play 100 league games for the club.

The oldest player ever to make his debut for Norwich City in a Football League game did so on 25th August 1923 in a 1-1 draw with Millwall at the Nest. His name was Albert Sturgess and he was nearly 41 years old. He came to Norwich via Sheffield United and Stoke City and made two full international appearances for England. He played at full-back and straight away became team captain and went on to make 52 first-team appearances.

But the oldest player ever to make his full debut for Norwich was 41-year-old Hugh McQueen who played only one game for the team on 15th March 1909 in a 6-1 defeat at Rotherham. A former first teamer for Liverpool, he was actually employed by the club as a trainer, but injuries to first-team players led to him having to play.

–LEGENDS–

Joe Hannah

Joe Hannah was a Norfolk boy through and through; born in Sheringham in 1898 he would go on to become one of the most loved Norwich City players of the era, appearing 427 times, a record beaten only by Kevin Keelan, Ron Ashman, Dave Stringer and Bryan Gunn. His debut came in January 1921 against Newport and he continued to play for another 14 years. He played in more than half the games of the Division Three South programme of 1933–34, when Norwich won the championship. Hannah holds fifth place in the list of all-time appearances for Norwich City, something unlikely to change in the modern era.

FOOTBALL –STATS–

Joe Hannah

Name: James Henry Hannah

Born: Sheringham, 30th November 1898

Died: Stepney, 1st February 1975

Position: Centre-half and full-back

Norwich City Playing Career: 1921–35

Club Appearances: 427

Goals: 21

"*Legend has it that Hannah was once so annoyed with his performance, he walked home from Norwich to Sheringham as a punishment.*"

Norwich Evening News reports after one of Hannah's poorer performances

Making an Impression

For a short time the Canaries wore white shirts; here they can be seen during a team photo for the 1924–25 season.

When you start a new job you want to make an impression. It's the same for a football club joining a new league. When Norwich joined Division Three in 1920 they achieved the very opposite. After a 1-1 draw at Plymouth and another 1-1 draw at Exeter, it was downhill all the way. Two more draws followed in home matches against the same teams. So far, so good. Unfortunately, the Canaries contrived to lose their next five games, including a 5-2 away debacle at Swansea. By this time Norwich were bottom of the league. It was only in their 14th game that they scraped a 1-0 win against Reading. Three more consecutive wins lifted the club up to 14th place, but it was not enough to save manager Charlie O'Hagan's job. He was replaced by Albert Gosnell, who stabilized things, and in the end the club finished in 16th place.

From the 1920–21 season, Division Three would prove to be Norwich City's home for 27 out of the next 32 seasons. For the first season it was a single league, but from 1922–23 it was split into Division Three North and Division Three South.

The Canaries' first match in Division Three South came on 27th August 1921 in a home game against Luton. It was not a successful start. They lost 1-0 and ended up finishing the season in 15th place. Indeed, at no time in the 1920s did Norwich manage to climb above halfway.

ABOVE: Albert Arthur Gosnell was appointed manager on 8th January 1921.

In 1923, a decision was made to change the club strip and yellow was dropped as the main colour on the team shirts. There were a lot of new players joining the club and the board had also changed so the change of strip was seen as signifying a new era. But little changed over the following years on the pitch, with the team remaining a relatively insignificant Division Three South team.

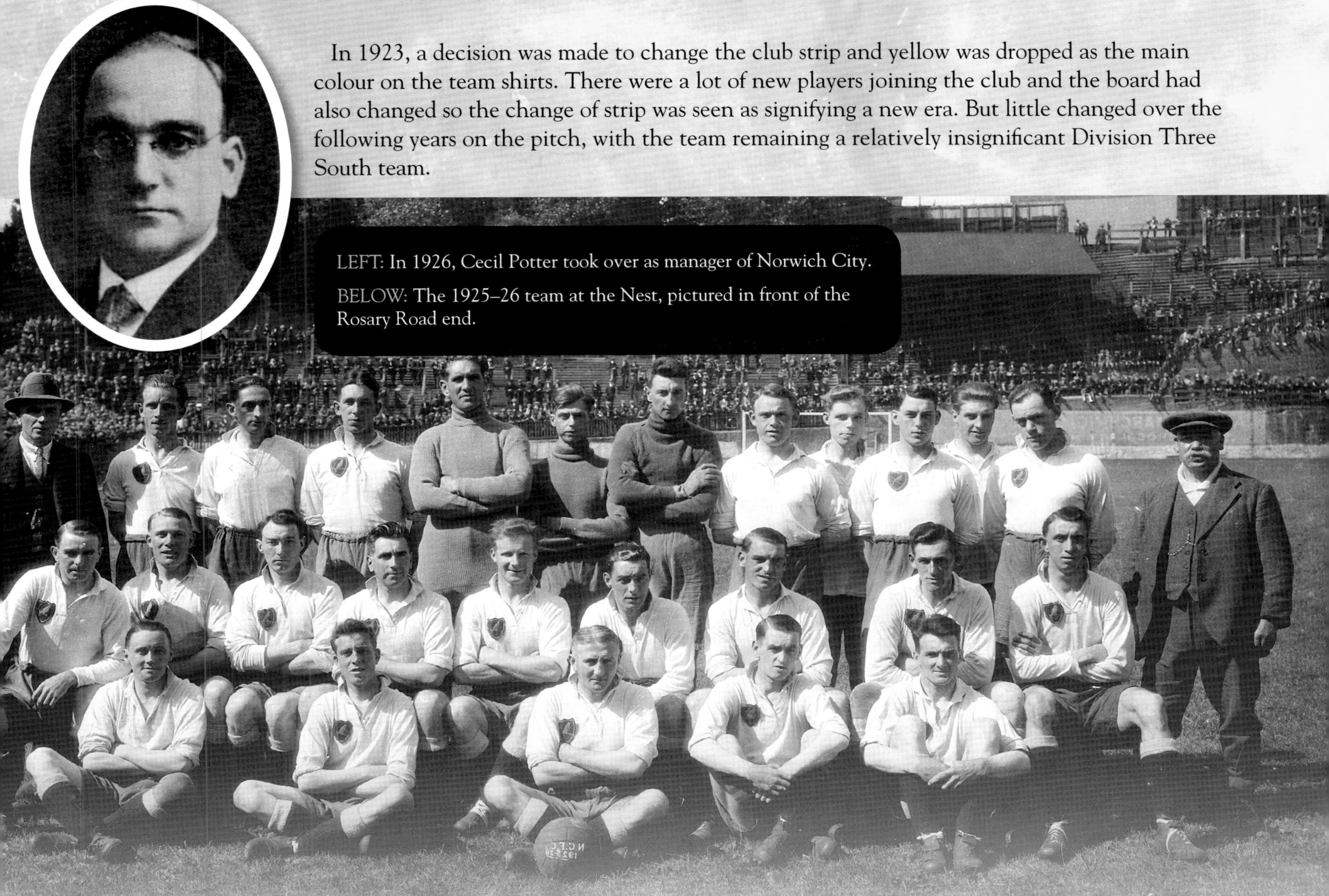

LEFT: In 1926, Cecil Potter took over as manager of Norwich City.

BELOW: The 1925–26 team at the Nest, pictured in front of the Rosary Road end.

The 1925–26 season saw the end of Albert Gosnell's reign and James Stansfield was recalled to take the helm, but he lasted only a few months before pre-war centre-forward Cecil Potter returned to the Nest as manager. In his two seasons in charge the club were constantly fighting to remain above the re-election zone.

In 1928–29 Norwich met the Corinthians in the third round of the FA Cup and the match produced what many at the time believed to be the best display of football ever seen at the Nest. More than 20,000 fans packed into the ground to witness the Corinthians teach Norwich a lesson they weren't to forget for many years. Five goals without reply went crashing into the City goal. This, and a defeat a week later at home by Charlton Athletic, was enough to encourage manager Cecil Potter to resign.

Cecil Potter will, however, forever be remembered as the manager who signed a striker called Percy Varco from Queens Park Rangers. Varco's career was restricted by injury and he only played 65 games for the Canaries. But what memories he left. He scored an astonishing 47 goals in those games, including 10 in his first seven and finished his first season with a haul of 32. The crowd would regularly cry "Give it to Varco", a chant which was heard at the Nest long after his departure on a free transfer to Exeter City in 1930.

Into the 1930s

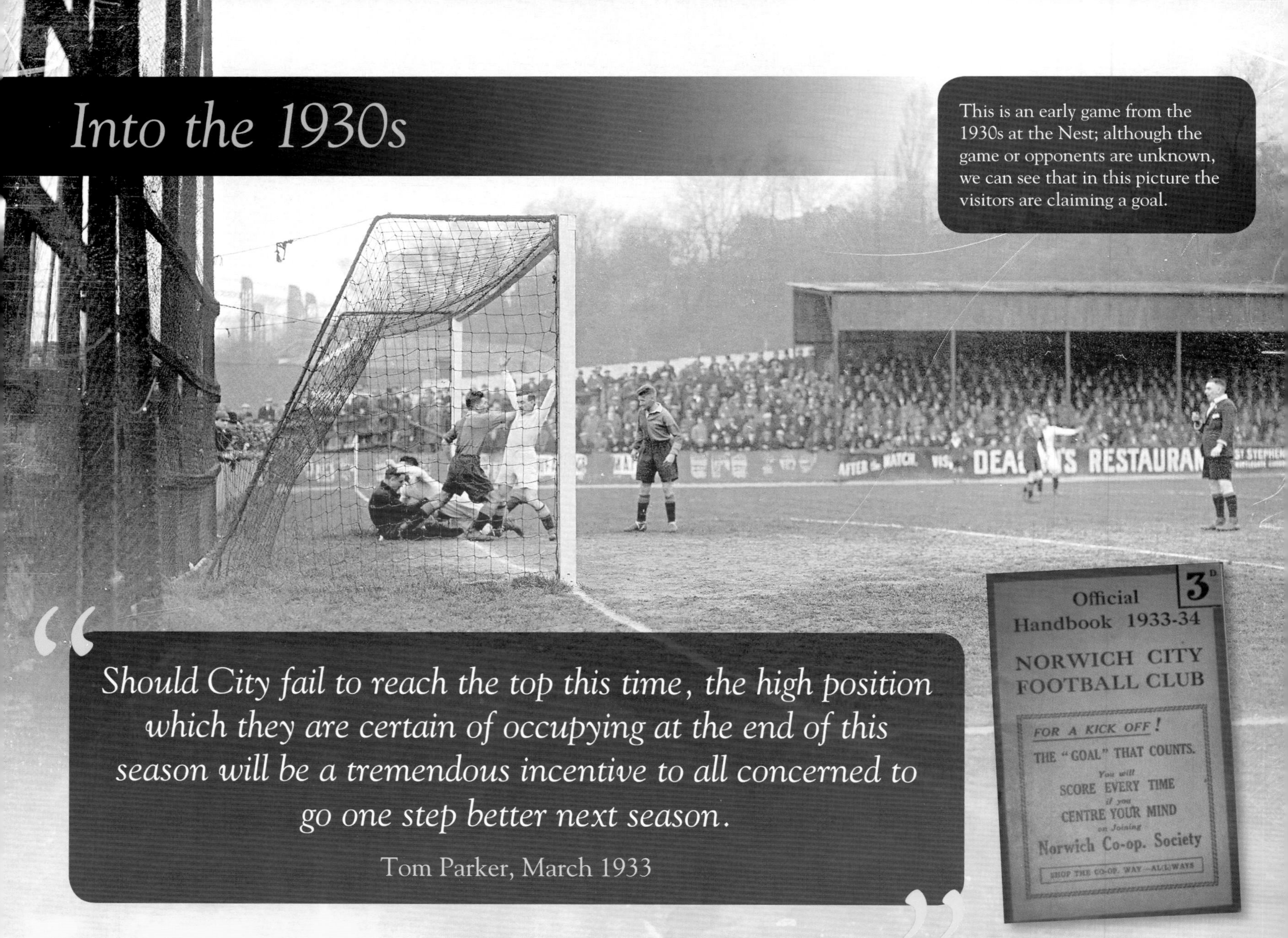

This is an early game from the 1930s at the Nest; although the game or opponents are unknown, we can see that in this picture the visitors are claiming a goal.

> *"Should City fail to reach the top this time, the high position which they are certain of occupying at the end of this season will be a tremendous incentive to all concerned to go one step better next season."*
>
> Tom Parker, March 1933

It was only in 1929–30 that the team's fortunes seemed to be turning. Newly appointed manager Jimmy Kerr inspired an eighth place finish, but it proved illusory. Luckily for Norwich there was no relegation system from either of the Division Three leagues, as the following season the Canaries suffered the humiliation of finishing bottom, which was hardly surprising as they started a run of 21 consecutive away defeats – a record that holds to this day. But only three seasons later, promotion to the big time, well, semi-big time, beckoned. Or at least that is how it seemed for much of the season. It nearly came in 1932–33 but in the end the Canaries missed out, finishing third. In those days only the champions were promoted. Sadly, Jim Kerr did not live to see the fruits of his work and suddenly died in February 1933. Tom Parker was hastily appointed as manager and it was he who led Norwich to their first promotion at the end of the 1933–34 season, winning the Division Three South Championship. He brought in Arsenal full-back Billy Warnes, Sunderland centre-forward Jack Vinall as well as Darlington centre-half Tom Halliday, all of whom played a key part in the push for promotion.

–LEGENDS–

Bernard Robinson

Bernard Robinson was one of City's most popular players with an amazing service spanning 17 years. His total of 380 appearances places him 12th in the club's all-time appearance table, and if it had not been for the outbreak of war it is likely that he would have gone on to become the club's record appearance maker. He joined Norwich City as a 19-year-old from King's Lynn, spotted by the then manager Jimmy Kerr. Robinson was a key player in the team that won the Division Three South Championship of 1934, and finally bowed out in March 1949, fittingly after a local derby victory over Ipswich. Robinson went on to live into his nineties, taking part in most of the club's centenary celebrations, recalling his time at the Nest, Carrow Road, and during the Second World War.

"It should never have been a football ground and I was glad to get away from the place – it was a wicked ground. At one end of the ground it just went straight up and to stop all the earth coming down on to the pitch they had a huge cement wall. It was five or six feet from the touchline so wingers had to be careful. Behind the other goal were the dressing rooms and a small stand and apart from that there was just a row of houses and the gardens were 15 to 20 feet below the level of the pitch. There was a big wire netting fence to stop the ball going in there. It was very dangerous."

Former Norwich City defender Bernard Robinson talking to the *Eastern Daily Press* about the Nest, at the age of 90

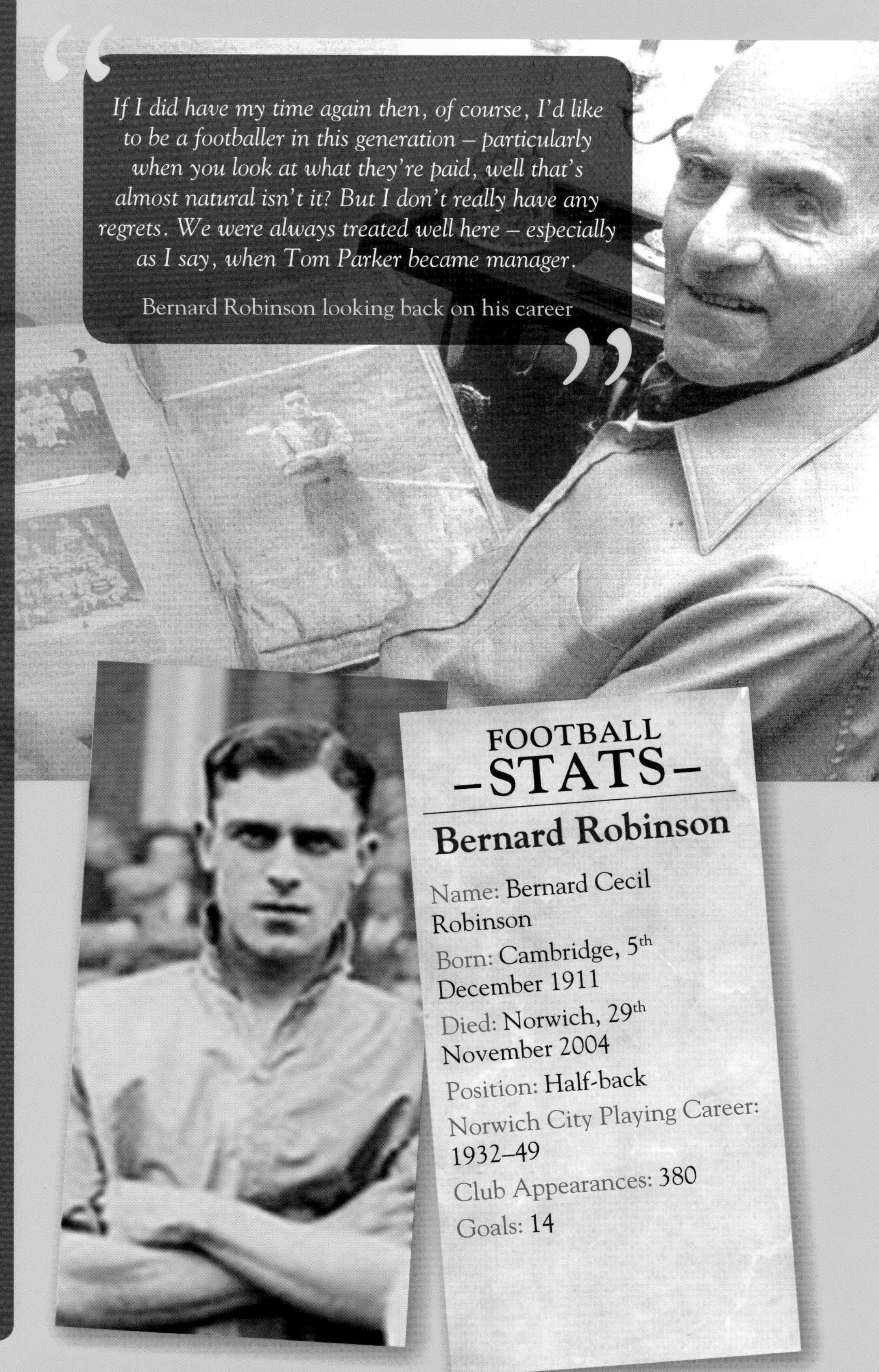

"If I did have my time again then, of course, I'd like to be a footballer in this generation – particularly when you look at what they're paid, well that's almost natural isn't it? But I don't really have any regrets. We were always treated well here – especially as I say, when Tom Parker became manager."

Bernard Robinson looking back on his career

FOOTBALL –STATS–

Bernard Robinson

Name: Bernard Cecil Robinson

Born: Cambridge, 5th December 1911

Died: Norwich, 29th November 2004

Position: Half-back

Norwich City Playing Career: 1932–49

Club Appearances: 380

Goals: 14

Promotion Beckons

The Canaries' line-up for the 1932–33 season. Back row (left to right): Bernard Robinson, Joe Hannah, Robert Robinson, Bob Young (trainer), Stan Ramsay, Doug Lochhead. Front row: Ken Burditt, Tom Scott, Tom Williamson, Oliver Brown, Cec Blakemore, Lionel Murphy.

One of the key matches in the 1933–34 promotion-winning season came at the Nest on 21st April 1934 between Norwich, who were already topping the table, and second-placed Coventry City. Norwich had been on an unbeaten run which had already stretched to 16 games before a 1-0 defeat in the previous game away to Reading.. But a win for Norwich against Coventry City would guarantee promotion.

It had been an astonishing season and it began with the Canaries starting as they meant to go on, with an unbeaten five-match run. There was a 5-2 away setback at QPR, but after that Norwich only lost three further games that season. Having gone top at the beginning of November, apart from one week in early January, they stayed there for the rest of the season.

Now, nearly 17,000 excited fans packed into the Nest to witness the Canaries beating the Sky Blues 3-1 with goals from Jack Vinall, Ken Burditt and Sam Bell. And that meant they were champions and promoted to Division Two for the first time in the club's history. Captained by Stan Ramsay, they scored 88 goals (56 goals were shared between Vinall, Warnes and Burditt) and kept 16 clean sheets. This was the team which clinched the title…

Norwich Team: Norman Wharton, Albert Thorpe, Stan Ramsay, Robert Morris, Tom Halliday, Doug Lochhead, Sam Bell, Ken Burditt, Jack Vinall, Harold Houghton, Lionel Murphy.

Season Stats 1933–34

Jack Vinall **(42 appearances)**
Norman Wharton **(42 appearances)**
Tom Halliday **(40 appearances)**
Lionel Murphy **(39 appearances)**
Billy Warnes **(39 appearances)**
Stan Ramsay **(38 appearances)**
Ken Burditt **(37 appearances)**
Bernard Robinson **(33 appearances)**
Doug Lochhead **(31 appearances)**
Joe Hannah **(26 appearances)**
Albert Thorpe **(20 appearances)**
Thomas Scott **(17 appearances)**
Harold Houghton **(11 appearances)**
William Smith **(11 appearances)**
Sam Bell **(10 appearances)**
Theo Pike **(8 appearances)**
Rod Williams **(8 appearances)**
Robert Morris **(6 appearances)**
Alf Kirchen **(1 appearance)**
Frank Perfect **(1 appearance)**
Tom Williamson **(1 appearance)**
Gordon Wilson **(1 appearance)**

Record: P42 W25 D11 L6 F88 A49 PTS61
Goals: Vinall 21, Warnes 21, Burditt 14, Scott 9, Murphy 7, Williams 6, Bell 3, Pike 3, Houghton 2, Lochhead 1, Williamson 1
Manager: Tom Parker

LEFT: On Thursday 4th April 1929, Jimmy Kerr was appointed manager.

BELOW: After the sad death of Jimmy Kerr, Tom Parker was appointed manager in March 1933.

BOTTOM: The Canaries' cup record in the 1930s was certainly not anything to write home about. Only once in 1934–35 did Norwich reach the fifth round, and then they were beaten 1-0 by Sheffield Wednesday.

–LEGENDS–

Percy Varco

Although Percy Varco was at the club for just two and a half years, he remains a true legend to this day. Before he joined Norwich City he had played for Torquay, Aston Villa and Queens Park Rangers. His strike rate was brilliant; he scored seven goals in his first 10 league games. By the time he left City on Boxing Day 1929 he had achieved 47 goals in 65 appearances; a week later he joined Exeter on a free transfer. After his retirement from the game he became a fish merchant and later Mayor of Fowey.

FOOTBALL –STATS–

Percy Varco

Name: Percy Varco
Born: Fowey, 17th April 1904
Died: Fowey, 29th January 1982
Position: Forward
Norwich City Playing Career: 1927–29
Club Appearances: 65
Goals: 47

Varco at the launch of 'On the Ball, City' in 1972.

–LEGENDS–

Billy Furness

Billy Furness is one of the few Norwich City players who played for England; he was capped by England against Italy in May 1933. He had made his name at Leeds United in the early 1930s, but in 1937 Norwich City snapped him up for £2,750. Unfortunately, like many great players, war got in his way, and by the time he retired he had scored 21 times in 96 appearances. Furness remained loyal to the club and later served as the trainer and physiotherapist, before he died in Norwich aged 71.

FOOTBALL –STATS–

Billy Furness

Name: William Isaac Furness

Born: Washington, Co Durham, 8th June 1909

Died: Norwich, 29th August 1980

Position: Inside-forward

Norwich City Playing Career: 1937–46

Club Appearances: 96

Goals: 21

England Caps: 1

By the beginning of the 1930s the club's directors knew that their time at the Nest needed to draw to a close. The ground was becoming shabby and if the Canaries wanted to progress it was inevitable that they would need to build a new ground. The situation was brought to a head on 15th May 1935 when the FA wrote to the club saying they were concerned that the Nest wasn't suitable for games which would attract large crowds.

Ten days later the club accepted an offer of an alternative site near to the main railway station at Thorpe, less than a mile away from the Nest. Construction began immediately and what became known locally as the "Eighth wonder of the world", the Carrow Road ground, came into being within three months.

There were three sides of open terraces and one covered stand, with a Colman's Mustard advert daubed on the roof in white

City meet Grimsby Town in the Hospital Cup final on 7th May 1934 at the Nest.

paint. It wasn't until 1956 that floodlights were built at a cost of £9,000. Incredibly, that expense nearly bankrupted the club. Later, the 1959 FA Cup run provided funds for the South Stand to have a roof.

"For years the dire need of an up-to-date ground with adequate room and round the pitch, and with ample accommodation for the growing band of supporters, had been fully recognised in the boardroom. Several sites had been under review, yet a solution of the problem seemed as far off as ever."

"Canary", *Eastern Daily Press*

The New Era Begins

Russell Colman, president of Norwich City FC, officially opening the grounds at Carrow Road.

The club's first home game at their new ground came on 31st August 1935, at the start of the 1935–36 season. A crowd just shy of 30,000 packed into Carrow Road to witness an exciting 4-3 win over West Ham United. Doug Lochhead secured his place in the annals of Canaries' history by scoring the first goal at Carrow Road. Although attendances fluctuated over the course of the season, the 30,000 barrier was finally broken when 32,378 spectators watched the 1-1 draw against Chelsea in the third round of the FA Cup in January 1936.

BELOW: One of the only remaining colour pictures of Carrow Road in 1935.

> *Jubilee Year, 1935, will ever be looked back to in the annals of local sport as the year in which the City, brought face to face with the absolute necessity of finding a new home, built and equipped one for themselves in far less time than can seldom have been attempted by a big club.*
>
> "Canary", *Eastern Daily Press*

A Royal Visit

ABOVE: History was made when King George VI attended the City v Millwall game of October 1938. It was the first time a reigning monarch had visited a Division Two match. A pity he left after only 15 minutes!

In February 1936 Jack Vinall scored the first hat-trick by a Norwich City player at Carrow Road. It came in a 5-1 trouncing of Southampton.

Later that season, Norwich City played three matches in four days across the Easter weekend. For the era, this was nothing unusual, but it's interesting to note that nine players played in all three games, and remember, there were no substitutes at that time. For the record the Canaries won two and drew the other game.

The first three seasons Norwich spent in Division Two were relatively successful. Although they were never going to contend for promotion, staving off relegation back to Division Three was the most important thing. This they did very successfully, finishing 14th and 11th. But in 1937–38 this changed. Inexplicably, midway through the season Tom Parker left the club for Southampton and the board appointed a new manager in Arthur "Jimmy" Jewell. This was unbelievable because not only had Jewell never managed before, he hadn't played the game either. Imagine the reaction if today's Norwich City appointed Graham

ABOVE: Tom Smalley, City captain, is shown here introducing his players to the King.

Poll as manager – well that's what Norwich did, for Jimmy Jewell was one of the better known referees of his time. Indeed, he had refereed the FA Cup final less than a year before. His appointment proved something of a disaster. In his 20 games in charge only six resulted in wins. In the end Norwich only needed three points from their last two games to survive, but it was not to be. John Milburn missed a penalty at Plymouth and in the last match against fellow relegation contenders Nottingham Forest Norwich needed to win by four clear goals but could only manage one. They went down by 0.05 of a goal in the days when goal average counted.

ABOVE: Bob Young was appointed as manager in 1937.

RIGHT: Jimmy Jewell was Norwich's last manager before the outbreak of war.

Cup Glory 1939-1959

Carrow Road, with only the Main Stand and the Barclay covered.

Football Resumes after the War

ABOVE: The Norwich City line-up for the 1947–48 season. Back row (left to right): Bert Holmes, Bernard Robinson, Allenby Driver, Norman Low, Ken Nethercott, Don Edwards, Derek Davis, Grenville Williams, Jimmy Guy, Leslie Dawes, Maurice Tobin. Middle row: Billy Furness (assistant trainer), Fred Mansfield, Denis Morgan, Trevor Rowlands, Oscar Hold, Albert Foan, Johnny Church, Ivan Armes, Eric Arnold, Leslie Eyre, Fred Hall ("A" team trainer). Front row: Don Pickwick, Len Dutton, Noel Kinsey, Harry Proctor (trainer), Doug Lochhead (manager), Peter Dash (secretary), Terry Ryder, Sid Jones, George Morgan. Seated in front: Maldwyn Reed, Denys Jones.

In theory Norwich returned to Division Three South at the start of the 1939–40 season, but even though three matches had already been played, league football was suspended upon the outbreak of war in early September 1939 and they are expunged from the records. In fact three matches had already been played, but they were expunged from league records. Matches were then organized on a regional basis, and played as friendlies. Bob Young once again became manager, and Bill Shankly even turned out for the Canaries on three occasions, playing under the pseudonym of A Newman.

Norwich played West Ham United in a 1940–41 Football League War Cup competition, but lost 5-3 on aggregate.

In general, the war years were not kind to the club. The odd highlight, like an 18-0 win against Brighton on Christmas Day 1940, masked the troubled times which lay ahead. Matches continued to be played, but inevitably, without the league or cup to play for, finances suffered. When the club's shareholders were summoned together in August 1945 they were met with the news that the club owed nearly £12,000 in loans, nearly £6,000 to various creditors and were £11,000 overdrawn at the bank.

And so it was that Norwich City resumed their Division Three South career, with new team manager Cyril Spiers, at the start of the 1946–47 season. It spelled the start of another long stint in the division, until promotion to Division Two eventually came in May 1960. These were not happy times for the club. In the first two seasons the Canaries finished second from bottom.

Cyril Spiers managed Norwich for less than two years, before going back to manage Cardiff midway through the 1947–48 season, but he was a talented administrator and talent spotter. Under his reign Ron Ashman, Ken Nethercott, Don Pickwick, Denis Morgan, Leslie Eyre and Noel Kinsey were all given their debuts. All of them made more than 200 appearances for the Canaries. In short, he got the club back on its financial feet and ensured it would still be in existence as the 1950s got underway.

Things started looking up in the 1949–50 season with a 11th place finish. It was also the season in which manager Doug Lochhead gave young Irish forward Johnny Gavin his debut. Gavin went on to score 132 goals in 338 appearances during his two spells at the club, and remains the club's all-time top scorer.

RIGHT: Norwich fans at Carrow Road hoping to get a view of the Portsmouth game on 12th January 1950. Norwich were defeated 2-0.

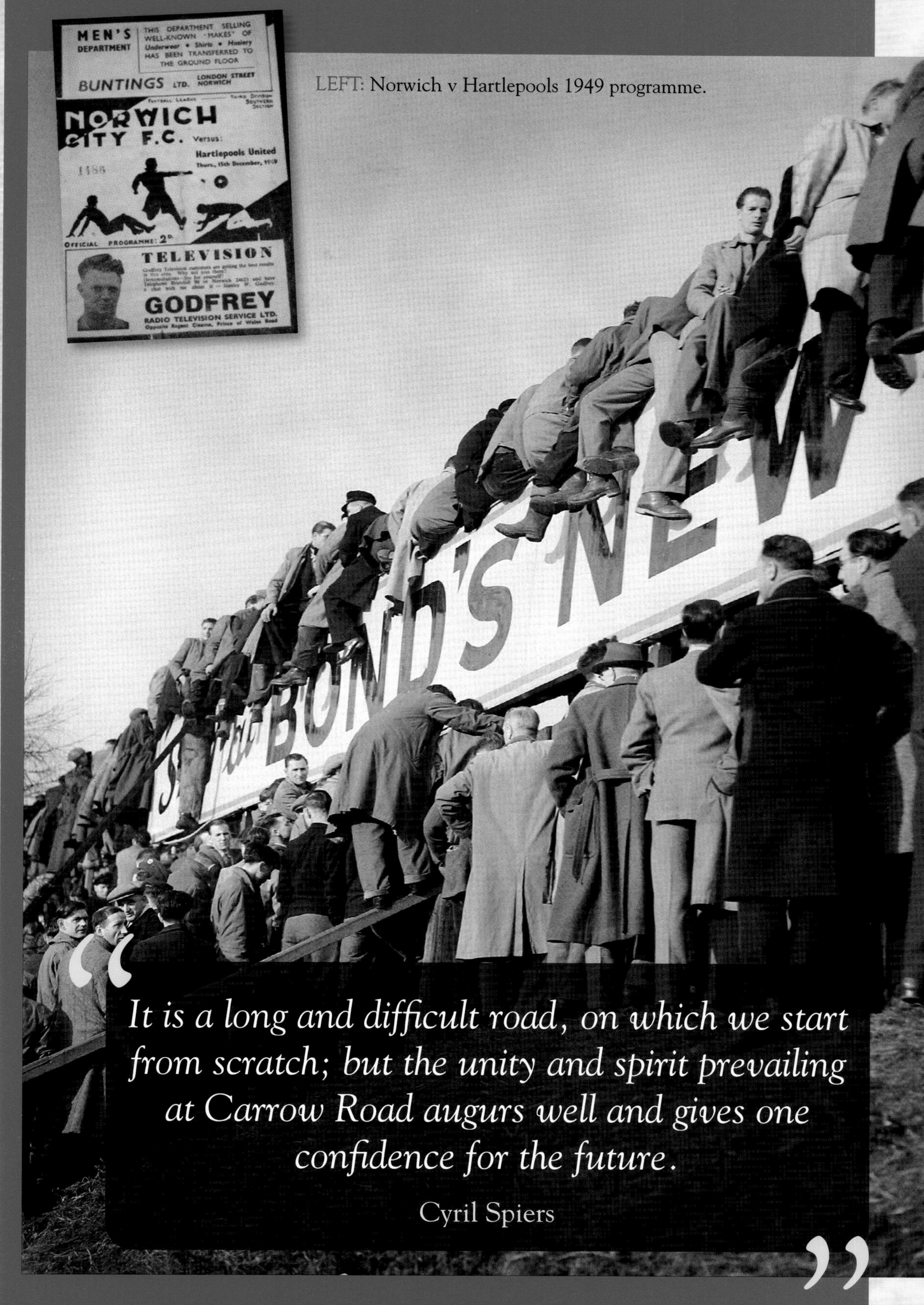

LEFT: Norwich v Hartlepools 1949 programme.

"It is a long and difficult road, on which we start from scratch; but the unity and spirit prevailing at Carrow Road augurs well and gives one confidence for the future."

Cyril Spiers

Despite their dismal few years, Norwich City were attracting huge crowds. In 1950–51 their average attendance was 24,700 – astonishing for a team languishing in the nether regions of Division Three South. By this time Lochhead had been succeeded as manager by City defender Norman Low. He led the team to successive finishes of second, third and fourth as well as an FA Cup fourth-round win against Liverpool in 1951 – a match which became known as "Docherty's Match". The popular winger scored two goals and dominated the game. The following season saw Norwich record their biggest ever win at Carrow Road – 8-0 over Walsall, with Roy Hollis scoring five. The following season they beat Shrewsbury 8-1 away. It was during the 1951–52 season that a young player called Roy McCrohan signed from Reading. He would be a lynchpin of the team for the rest of the decade and his 426 appearances put him in sixth place in the club's all-time appearance league table.

ABOVE: This picture was taken at Volendam on 21st May 1952, during City's four-match tour of Holland. Back row (left to right): Harry Proctor (trainer), Ron Ashman, Johnny Gavin, Denis Morgan, Reg Foulkes, Noel Kinsey, Len Dutton and Norman Low (manager). Front row: Bill Lewis, Don Pickwick, Ken Nethercott, Roy Hollis and John Summers.

12th January 1952. Norwich City 0 Arsenal 5.

LEFT & BELOW & BOTTOM: 6th January 1951. Action from Norwich v Liverpool. Norwich won 3-1.

All-Time Top Appearances

1 Kevin Keelan **673**
2 Ron Ashman **662**
3 David Stringer **499**
4 Bryan Gunn **477**
5 Joe Hannah **427**
6 Roy McCrohan **426**
7 Ian Crook **418**
8 Ken Nethercott **416**
9 Mark Bowen **399**
10 Terry Allcock **389**
11 Craig Fleming **382**
12 Bernard Robinson **380**
13 Ian Culverhouse **369**
14 Duncan Forbes **357**
15 Daryl Sutch **352**
16 Adam Drury **350***
17 Barry Butler **349**
18 Graham Paddon **340**
19 Johnny Gavin **338**
20 George Martin **337**

* still playing

Giant-killing

The 1953–54 season may have been a disappointment in the league (the club finished seventh) but it was memorable for one match in particular – a fourth-round FA Cup match at Highbury. Arsenal were League Champions and were expected to sweep past Norwich in their quest for cup glory. It didn't quite turn out like that. Norwich were awarded a penalty in the second minute, but Bobby Brennan, who had been signed from Fulham for a club record £15,000 earlier in the season, missed. Half an hour later Brennan was sent off, alongside Arsenal's Alex Forbes. Arsenal scored the first goal, but two goals from Tom Johnston saw Norwich achieve their greatest ever cup win.

RIGHT: One of the Canaries' most unlikely FA Cup triumphs, when City defeated Arsenal 2-1 at Highbury on 30th January 1954.

RIGHT: Lewis and Foulkes exhausted after the famous victory over Arsenal at Highbury in the fourth round of the FA Cup in 1954.

BELOW: Bobby Brennan scores for Norwich on 9th January 1954 in a 3-3 FA Cup third draw with Hastings United. The Canaries won the subsequent replay 3-0.

–LEGENDS–

Bobby Brennan

Bobby Brennan had previously played for Luton Town, Birmingham City and Fulham, but it was Carrow Road that made him a legend. He signed for Norwich from Fulham in 1953 for the pretty sum of £15,000.

Throughout his time at Norwich he made 250 appearances, scoring 52 goals, four of which were made during his time as part of the FA Cup giant-killing team of 1958–59. Brennan's ball skills took Norwich to the brink of a Wembley final, and he remains the only player to have scored for City in an FA Cup semi-final. He made his final league appearance in 1960, as Norwich won promotion to Division Two. After retiring as a player in April 1960, Brennan coached King's Lynn of the Southern League.

RIGHT: Bobby Brennan reading birthday telegrams on his 34th birthday in his dressing room. That day he had scored the only goal in the 1959 FA Cup semi-final v Luton Town.

FOOTBALL –STATS–

Bobby Brennan

Name: Robert Anderson Brennan

Born: Belfast, 14th March 1925

Died: Norwich, 1st January 2002

Position: Forward

Norwich City Playing Career: 1953–56, 1957–60

Club Appearances: 250

Goals: 52

Northern Ireland Caps: 5

Northern Ireland Goals: 1

20th March 1954, Norwich 1 Ipswich 2.

"There has been criticism of the fact that I let so many players go at the end of last season. My contention is that they were virtually 'dead wood' and were hindering the progress of younger, more promising men. In spite of his [Bobby Brennan's] undoubted abilities he was not a player to bring out the best in his colleagues."

Tom Parker, 1956

Despite occasional highs, the team's performance was on the wane. Norman Low had done a good job, but a 12th place finish in 1954–55 saw his five-year tenure brought to an abrupt end. Low, by all accounts, was bereft and must have been surprised to see the name of his successor. His name was Tom Parker, whose previous spell as Norwich manager had come 20 years earlier.

Parker's first signing was Ralph Hunt, an inside-forward from Bournemouth. In his first season Hunt scored a magnificent 33 goals. His contribution ensured a seventh place finish for the Canaries and he went on to score 72 goals in all, in 132 games. But this was a false dawn. Lack of transfer funds meant that many good players were released (like Bobby Brennan) and their replacements were of inferior quality.

All-Time Top Goalscorers

1 Johnny Gavin (1948–58) **132**
2 Terry Allcock (1958–69) **127**
3 Iwan Roberts (1997–2004) **96**
4 Robert Fleck (1987–92, 1995–98) **84**
5 Jack Vinall (1933–37) **80**
6 Ralph Hunt (1955–58) **72**
7 John Deehan (1981–86) **70**
8 Les Eyre (1946–51) **69**
9= Ron Davies (1963–66) **66**
9= Jimmy Hill (1958–63) **66**
9= Ted MacDougall (1973–76) **66**
12 Noel Kinsey (1947–53) **65**
13 Grant Holt (2009–) **62**
14 Ken Burditt (1931–36) **61**
15 Roy Hollis (1948–52) **59**
16= Kevin Drinkell (1985–88) **57**
16= Ken Foggo (1967–72) **57**
16= James Jackson (1923–27) **57**
19 Ron Ashman (1947–63) **56**
20 Tommy Bryceland (1962–69) **55**

Norman Low, Norwich City manager 1950–55.

The record has stood for a long time and I don't think that at the pace players are moving between clubs now that anyone will beat it.

Gavin on his goalscoring record

–LEGENDS–

Johnny Gavin

Johnny Gavin has gone down in history as the leading goalscorer in the club's history, with 132 goals in 338 appearances. An Irish player, he was bought at the bargain price of £1,500 from Limerick in 1948. His Canaries career was split into two halves; he originally scored 79 goals in 221 games before he joined Tottenham in 1954. But he returned a year later after an exchange deal with centre-half Maurice Norman, adding a further 53 goals to his record. After he retired from the game he went on to become a publican, and would often visit Carrow Road for players' reunions.

"Johnny was a very, very quick player, very brave, and brilliant in the air, considering he was not that tall. A lot of his goals were scored with his head. And remember, the ball we played with was a lot heavier in those days. He could jump as high as the crossbar and he wasn't afraid to get hurt – the number of times he would come in with blood on his shirt or he'd broken his nose. And 132 goals? Not bad for a winger."

Ken Nethercott

FOOTBALL –STATS–

Johnny Gavin

Name: John Thomas Gavin

Born: Limerick, 20th April 1928

Died: Cambridge, 20th September 2007

Position: Winger

Norwich City Playing Career: 1948–54, 1955–58

Club Appearances: 338

Goals: 132

Ireland Caps: 8

Ireland Goals: 2

Let There Be Light

The only illuminating point of the 1956–57 season was the switching on of the floodlights for the first time. Otherwise it was a time of unmitigated gloom, both on and off the pitch. Despite a reasonable start, a run of 25 matches without a win ensured Norwich finished right at the bottom of the pile. Re-election was a formality, but that season nearly proved to be the end of the road for the 55-year-old football club. Bankruptcy beckoned. Average attendances had dwindled to 10,000 and in December the local newspaper group had to step in to pay the players' wages. An Appeal Committee was formed with the task of raising £25,000 to save the club from financial ruin under the direction of the Lord Mayor Mr Arthur South – who would later go on to chair the club.

Tom Parker's contract was terminated and Bobby Brennan resigned from Great Yarmouth and returned to Norwich City, but the key appointment was that of Archie Macaulay as team manager. It was he who set the club on its way to better times.

ALL BRITISH BEERS
STEWARD & PATTESON LTD

Crisis!

The season 1957–58 was the final one of Division Three South. To ensure their place in the new Division Three the following season the Canaries needed to finish in 12th place or above, or suffer the indignity of being in the newly created Division Four. Sighs of relief came when they finished eighth. Attendances gradually rose and despite a lack of transfer funds Macaulay went back to his native Scotland and recruited a whole host of new players. Significantly, he also picked up Barry Butler from Sheffield Wednesday for £5,000 and Terry Allcock from Bolton. Each would go on to make more than 300 appearances and become Canary legends, with Allcock scoring 127 goals.

The following summer wingers Jimmy Hill (no, not that one) and Errol Crossan were signed from Newcastle and Southend respectively. Macaulay felt that he now had the players to mount a challenge, and he was proved right.

After only two seasons, the club achieved their first promotion in 26 years. It would be 50 years before they returned to Division Three.

Sunderland score in their 4-2 home defeat of Norwich City in the third round of the FA Cup, 7th January 1956.

> *The meeting itself was controlled by Mr South with the adroitness and skill of an elder statesman.*
>
> Ted Bell

ABOVE: On the 4th February 1957 at an Extraordinary General Meeting of City shareholders, a new board of directors was elected. Four of those directors are pictured here (left to right): Frederick Jex, James Hanly, George Fish and new chairman, Geoffrey Watling.

LEFT: Here Arthur South, the Lord Mayor of Norwich, is pictured chairing the EGM; he proved pivotal in City avoiding bankruptcy. South went on to serve the Canaries as chairman from 1973 to 1985.

BELOW: The ballot for five new directors of the board went on until nearly 1am, with the shareholders pictured considering their votes.

A Cup Run Like No Other

When a lower league side gets to the semi-finals of the FA Cup it is usually a fluke or just good luck. Norwich City's FA Cup run in 1959 was neither. Their attacking play won a lot of friends all over the country and they came very close to achieving their Wembley dream. The cup run still evokes a lot of memories among older Canaries – Bobby Brennan's wonder goal against Luton Town and Ken Nethercott playing on after dislocating his shoulder against Sheffield United are just two of the events which would count in any Top 100 list of Norwich City's Most Famous Moments.

Lying 18th in Division Three, few Canaries fans would have anticipated such a glorious cup round as City kicked off their first run tie on 15th November 1958 against non-league Ilford. Indeed, the near on 14,000 crowd were probably expecting the worst when Ilford scored the first goal in the 28th minute, but two second-half goals from Bobby Brennan and another from Jimmy Hill put Norwich through.

LEFT: One of the most successful City teams in their history. Here are the team that beat the mighty Manchester United in 1959.

The 1959 line-up that faced Luton in the FA Cup semi-final. Note the replacement of the injured Ken Nethercott with Sandy Kennon.

On to Round Two

The first of four replayed cup ties came in the second round against Swindon. A 1-1 draw at the County Ground saw a rematch at Carrow Road, with the reward being a glamorous third-round home tie against Manchester United. Norwich duly beat their Wiltshire opponents 1-0.

BELOW: 6th December 1958, Norwich 1 Swindon 1. Terry Bly in aerial combat with the Swindon goalkeeper.

Roy McCrohan

Roy McCrohan played for Norwich City for more than a decade, his debut came in 1951 as an inside-forward. However, he would go on to play in almost every position on the field throughout his career. His commitment and enthusiasm to the Canaries and his vital part in the 1959 cup run team have earned him a place in the Norwich City history books. After retirement from the game, he went into coaching, which eventually took him to the USA, where he still resides.

RIGHT: Roy McCrohan being handed his ticket at Norwich Thorpe station by Norwich's secretary Bert Westwood, before his team leaves for Sheffield in February 1959.

Roy McCrohan

Name: Roy McCrohan

Born: Reading, 22nd September 1930

Position: Right-half

Norwich City Playing Career: 1951–62

Club Appearances: 426

Goals: 23

The Glory of the Cup

Terry Bly and Errol Crossan enjoying a drink post match.

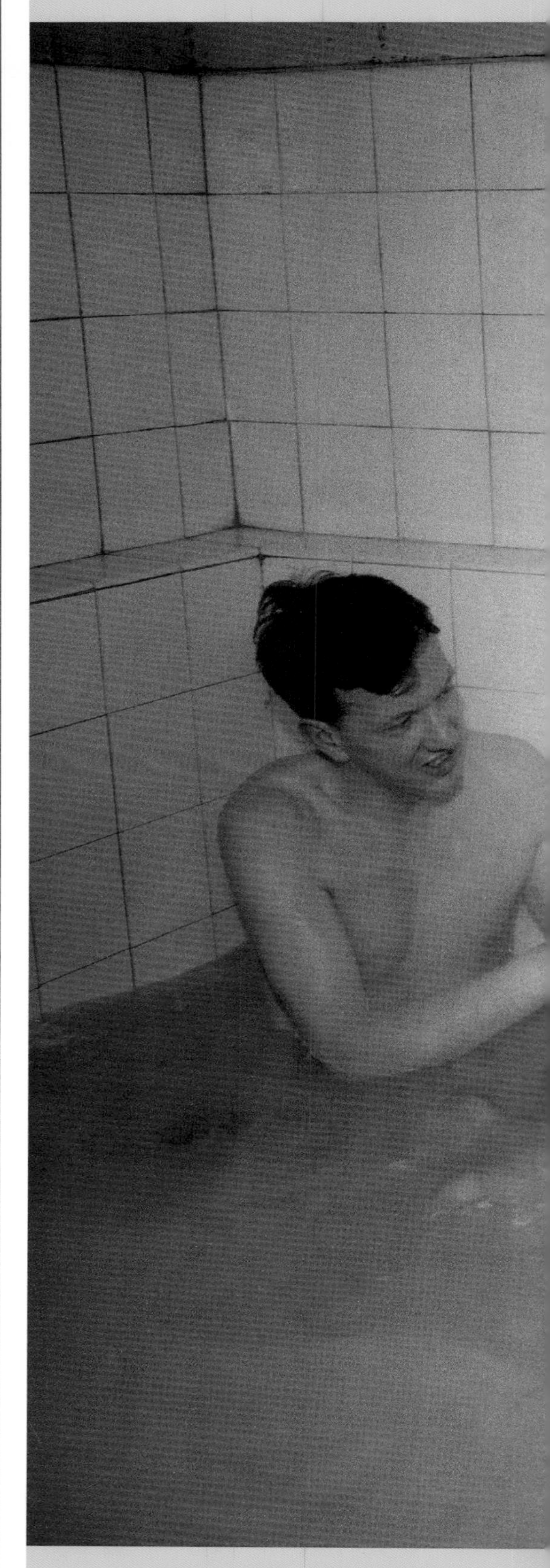

Matt Crowe, Sandy Kennon and Terry Allcock enjoying a bath in the players' dressing room during the cup run.

ABOVE: Terry Bly, one of Norwich's top strikers, admires his football boot.

BELOW: Injured keeper Ken Nethercott receiving a shoulder massage.

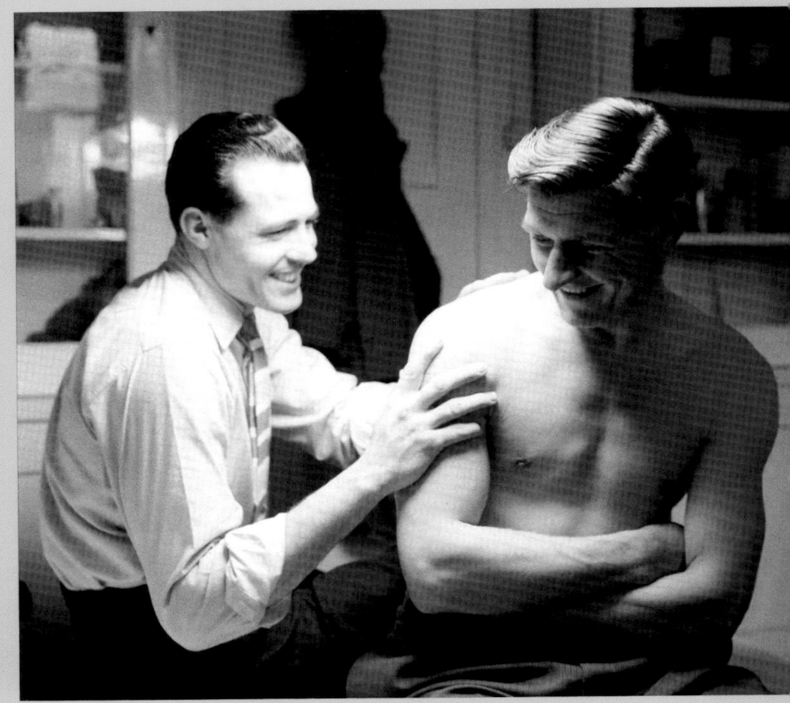

Round Three: Norwich 3 Manchester United 0

ABOVE: Terry Bly scores the opening goal.

Just over a month later the Busby Babes came to Norwich on the back of eight successive Division One wins, no doubt expecting to progress to the fourth round without too much trouble. The Canaries had other plans. They attacked the United defence relentlessly, with the City wing-halves causing havoc in the opposition defence. Terry Bly, with a brace, and Errol Crossan, scored the goals, but Bobby Brennan played a massive part in one of Norwich City's greatest performances of all time.

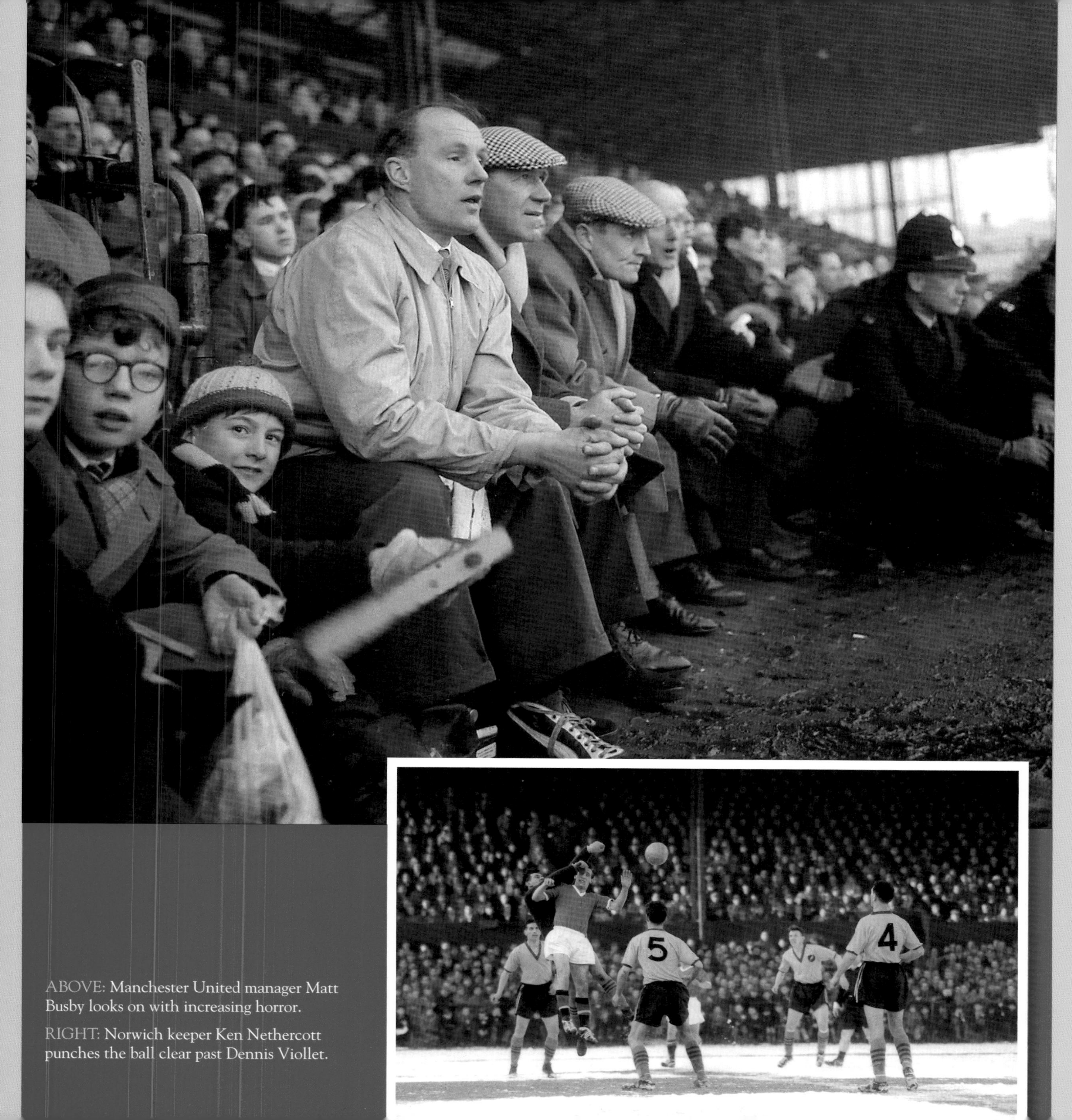

ABOVE: Manchester United manager Matt Busby looks on with increasing horror.

RIGHT: Norwich keeper Ken Nethercott punches the ball clear past Dennis Viollet.

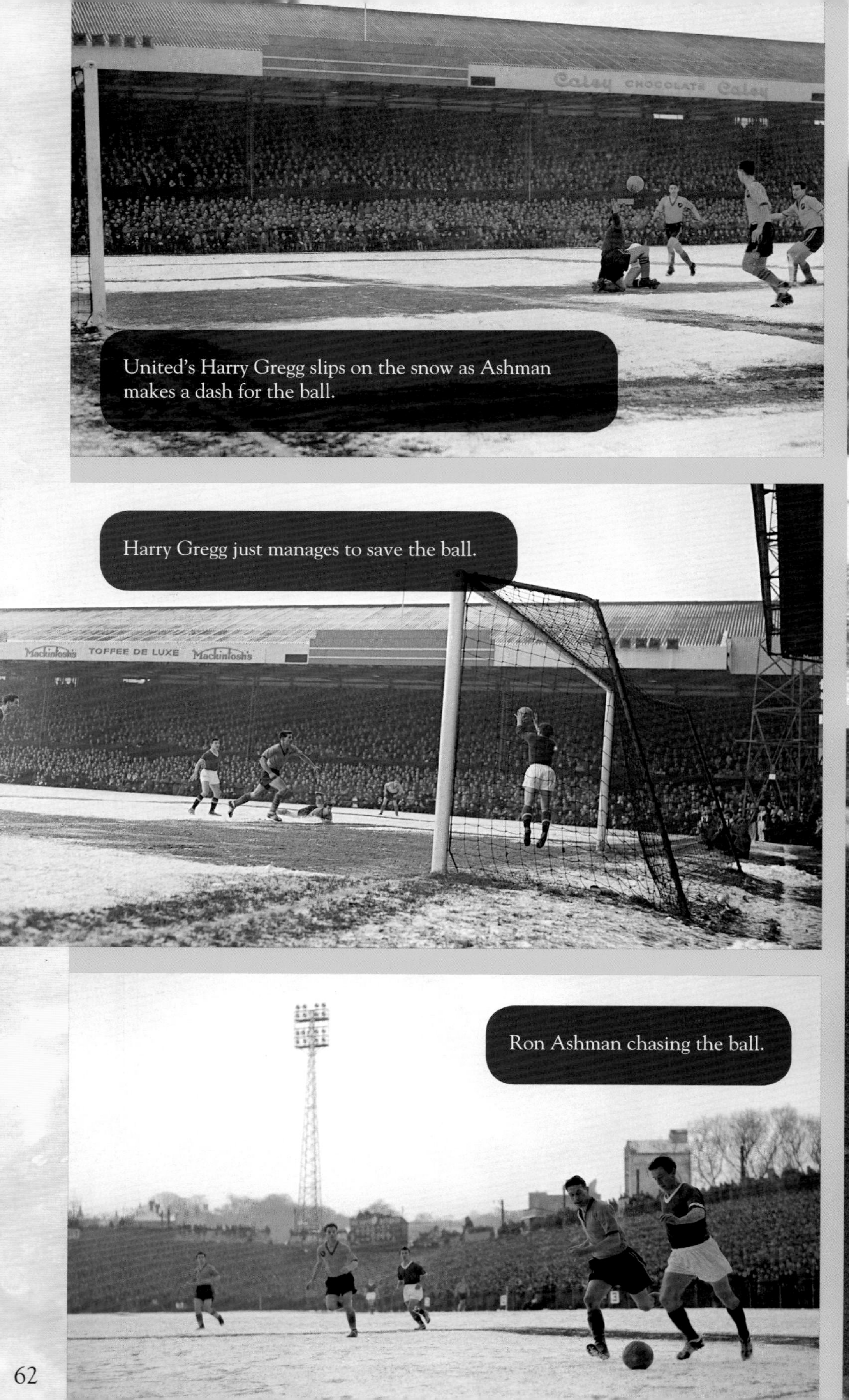

United's Harry Gregg slips on the snow as Ashman makes a dash for the ball.

Harry Gregg just manages to save the ball.

Ron Ashman chasing the ball.

Gregg watches in horror as Norwich score a goal.

Huge celebration from the crowd as the final whistle blows.

Round Four: Canaries v Bluebirds

On to the fourth round, and another home tie against Cardiff City. It proved to be a tough game for Norwich, as Cardiff took an early lead. Terry Bly and Errol Crossan, known as "The Twins" for their telepathic understanding, came to the rescue again, with Bly scoring a late netbuster with only three minutes remaining.

BELOW: 24th January 1959, Norwich 3 Cardiff City 2.

–LEGENDS–

Terry Bly

Originally Terry Bly joined Norwich City straight from school but was rejected by the club as not good enough. However, after proving himself by playing for Bury Town, he was welcomed back to Norwich in August 1956. He only made 67 appearances for the Canaries, scoring 38 goals, but this would have been higher if he wasn't blighted by a knee injury. He shot to national fame in the 1959 cup run, scoring twice in the famous 3-0 victory over Manchester United. *The Pink Un*'s headline even read "Bly, Bly Babes", a rather witty headline playing on Bly's achievements over Busby's Manchester United. Bly's success continued as he scored twice more against Cardiff City, another goal against the mighty Tottenham Hotspur, and a further two more as Sheffield United were overcome in the last eight. Bly was then sold to Peterborough in 1960 for £5,000; it was here he would gain the post-war record for the most goals in a season, netting 52 goals in the 1960–61 season.

FOOTBALL –STATS–

Terry Bly

Name: Terence Geoffrey Bly

Born: Fincham, 22nd October 1935

Died: Grantham, 24th September 2009

Position: Striker

Norwich City Playing Career: 1956–60

Club Appearances: 67

Goals: 38

"He was a very level-headed lad and deserved the success he had in his career. Although he was only at Norwich for a short while he made an immense contribution particularly in the Cup run."

Terry Allcock

14th February 1959, Spurs 1 Norwich 1. Future England centre-forward Bobby Smith lets fly but City goalkeeper Ken Nethercott matches his efforts.

Round Five: Valentine's Day Glory

Round five certainly earned Norwich City their spurs. Again Norwich had to triumph over adversity and win a replay at Carrow Road. The first leg against Tottenham took place at White Hart Lane on Valentine's Day. Some 20,000 Canary supporters made the 100-mile trek to north London. The cheers could be heard back in Norfolk when Terry Allcock put City ahead midway through a hard-fought second half. The minutes ticked by and it seemed that victory was in the bag, only for Spurs stalwart Cliff Jones to pop up in the last minute and earn Spurs a reprieve. But it was a reprieve the Lilywhites didn't make the most of in the replay five days later, despite the fact that Danny Blanchflower was brought into the line-up.

Thirty-eight thousand supporters packed into Carrow Road on a chilly Wednesday night. They had to wait until the 63rd minute for their beloved team to take the lead, when a seemingly skilful chip by Ron Ashman put Terry Bly through to score. Ashman revealed years later that his pass to Bly had in fact been a mistake. He had intended to spray the ball out to Bobby Brennan, but the ball hit his shin and found its way to Bly. On such chances do successful cup runs depend.

Spurs keeper John Hollowbread comes under pressure from Terry Allcock at White Hart Lane.

Norwich full-back Bryan Thurlow pursues Tottenham's Dave Dunmore.

City in despair as Spurs equalize in the final minute. Goalie Ken Nethercott and captain Ron Ashman are on the ground.

Triumph and Despair in the Sixth Round

On 28th February Norwich City met Sheffield United at Bramall Lane in the sixth round of the FA Cup. It was a bittersweet tie. In the 75th minute a brilliant goal from Errol Crossan after a mazy run from an in-form Bobby Brennan equalized United's second-minute opener. But the match will be remembered for an altogether different reason. Half an hour from the end stalwart goalkeeper Ken Nethercott dived at the feet of a Sheffield United striker to prevent a certain goal. He had dislocated his shoulder but was determined to play on. He never recovered and it was the last game he ever played for the club. The replay was a humdinger with the Canaries leading 2-0 at one stage and seemingly home and dry. Replacement goalkeeper Sandy Kennon, making his debut, then fumbled a cross and United clawed a goal back. But it was the irreplaceable Terry Bly who scored City's third and winning goal. The Blades got their second with seven minutes to go but the Canaries survived a hair-raising final few minutes to go through to the quarter-finals.

"I'm glad it was Sandy out there, not me; he's a much better keeper than I am."

Ken Nethercott after the replay

28th February 1959. Sheffield United 1 Norwich City 1.

EASTERN FOOTBALL NEWS

(THE PINK UN)

No. 1231—Twopence

Saturday, February 28, 1959

CITY STILL IN

Brennan lays on brilliant Crossan equaliser

NETHERCOTT PLAYS WITH SUSPECTED FRACTURE

SHEFFIELD UTD. .... 1 NORWICH CITY 1

NORWICH CITY are still in the Cup. With goalkeeper Ken Nethercott playing for most of the second half with a useless right arm, they gave a tremendous account of themselves against Sheffield United at Bramall Lane today and fully earned the right to entertain the Second Division side in a replay at Carrow Road next Wednesday.

This was a Cup-tie packed with drama and sparkling football. The Canaries found themselves a goal down before they had got used to the feel of the Bramall Lane pitch, and when half-time

ABOVE, BELOW & BOTTOM: Sheffield United's Hodgkinson fends off an attack from Terry Bly.

Norwich City FC captain, Ron Ashman, conducting phone interviews during the 1959 cup run.

ABOVE: Ken Nethercott's replacement, goalkeeper Sandy Kennon.

LEFT: A toast to celebrate the Canaries' victory over the Blades.

BELOW: 1959 manager, Archie Macaulay.

–LEGENDS–

Ken Nethercott

Arguably Ken Nethercott was Norwich City's all-time greatest goalkeeper, something he himself would never accept. He was signed by City manager Cyril Spiers, and made his first-team debut at Northampton in a Division Three South game in September 1947. He went on to play 416 games for City between 1947 and 1959, putting him eighth in the club's all-time appearance list. But he will go down in the history books for his heroism, in what turned out to be his last game. It was the 1959 FA Cup quarter-final at Sheffield United, with just half an hour remaining and Norwich down 1-0, when Nethercott dislocated his shoulder. This was before the days of substitutes and he insisted on playing to the end. It paid off: Norwich drew 1-1, and went on to win the subsequent replay.

FOOTBALL –STATS–

Ken Nethercott

Name: Kenneth Walter Samuel Nethercott

Born: Bristol, 22nd July 1925

Position: Goalkeeper

Norwich City Playing Career: 1947–59

Club Appearances: 416

Goals: 0

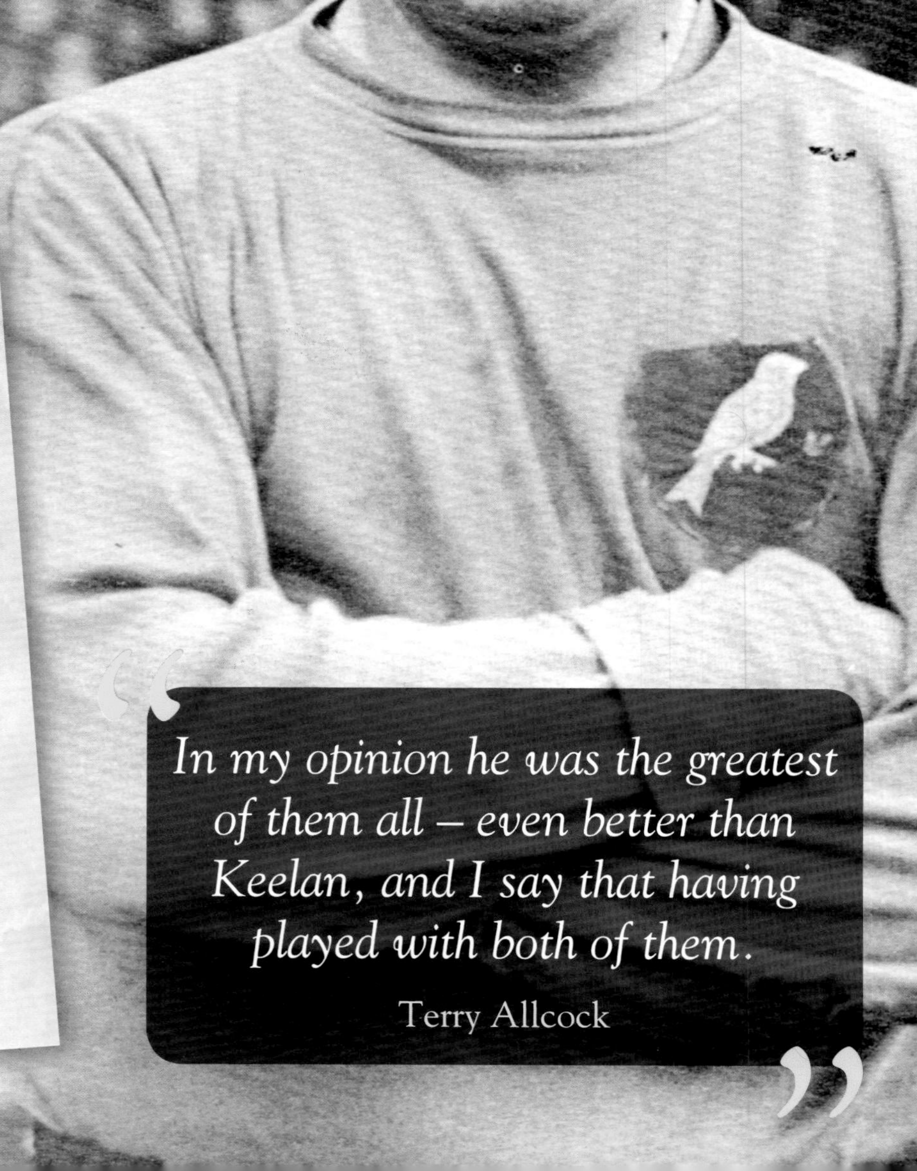

> *In my opinion he was the greatest of them all – even better than Keelan, and I say that having played with both of them.*
>
> Terry Allcock

One Match from Wembley

So the Canaries were potentially only 90 minutes away from Wembley Cup glory. And only the mighty Luton Town stood in their way. Luton, it has to be said, were no mugs, having reached Division One three years earlier. But the romantics were all behind the Division Three upstarts from Norfolk. The A11 was full of cars bedecked with yellow and blue, and trains were full of optimistic Canaries fans.

The tie took place on 14th March at White Hart Lane and the gods didn't seem to be with Norwich when Luton took the lead in the 35th minute. But Bobby Brennan netted in the 65th minute to pull Norwich level, and a series of outstanding saves by Sandy Kennon ensured that Luton were taken to a replay. In the rematch four days later at St Andrew's, Norwich kept to their recipe of attack, attack, attack, but failed to break down the Luton defence for the entire first half despite several near misses. But in the 56th minute Billy Bingham put the Hatters in front, and that proved to be the goal which sent Luton to Wembley and Norwich back to Norfolk.

> *Let me have the glory; give Ken Nethercott the medal. He deserves it.*
>
> Sandy Kennon, dreaming of Wembley glory

Allcock and Bly of Norwich go up with Pacey of Luton.

Terry Allcock collides with Luton's Ron Baynham.

Bly and Allcock are beaten by Luton's keeper, Baynham.

Norwich's Crossan heads wide.

Celebration

FA Cup 1958–59

First Round	15th November	H	Ilford	3–1	Hill, Brennan 2
Second Round	6th December	A	Swindon	1–1	Hill
	11th December	H	Swindon	1–0	Crossan
Third Round	10th January	H	Manchester United	3–0	Crossan, Bly 2
Fourth Round	24th January	H	Cardiff City	3–2	Crossan, Bly 2
Fifth Round	14th February	A	Tottenham	1–1	Allcock
	18th February	H	Tottenham	1–0	Bly
Sixth Round	28th February	A	Sheffield United	1–1	Crossan
	4th March	H	Sheffield United	3–2	Brennan, Bly 2
Semi-Finals	14th March	White Hart Lane	Luton Town	1–1	Brennan
	18th March	St Andrews	Luton Town	0–1	

LEFT: Crowds cheering on their Canary heroes as they make their way through Thorpe station.

BELOW: Brennan signs autographs as he travels in a special carriage on his return from Liverpool Street to Norwich.

Norwich City fans welcome their heroes.

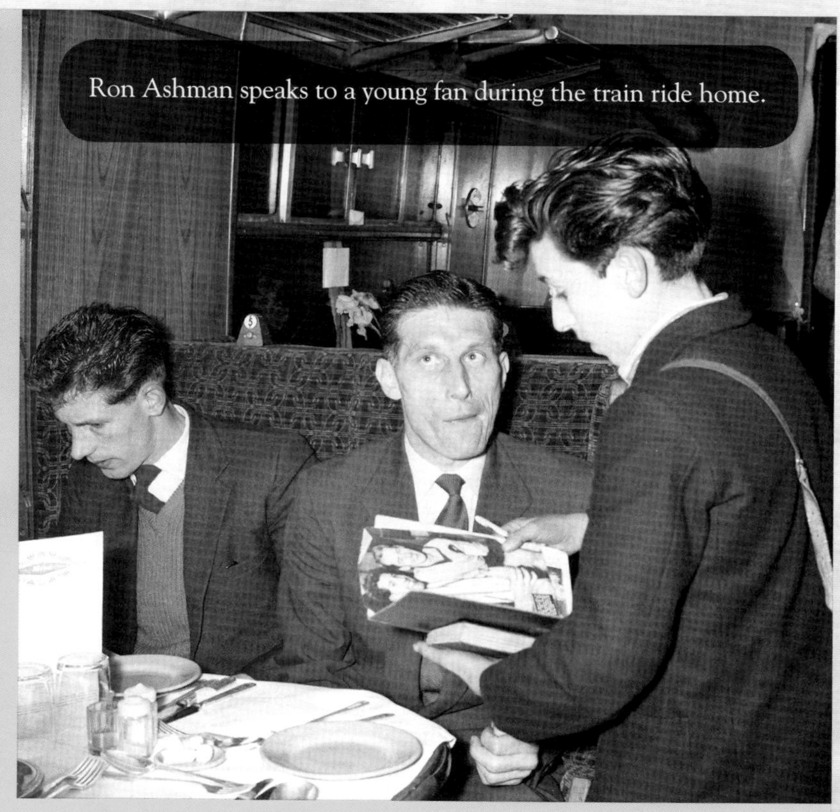
Ron Ashman speaks to a young fan during the train ride home.

Sandy Kennon relaxes in the special carriage home.

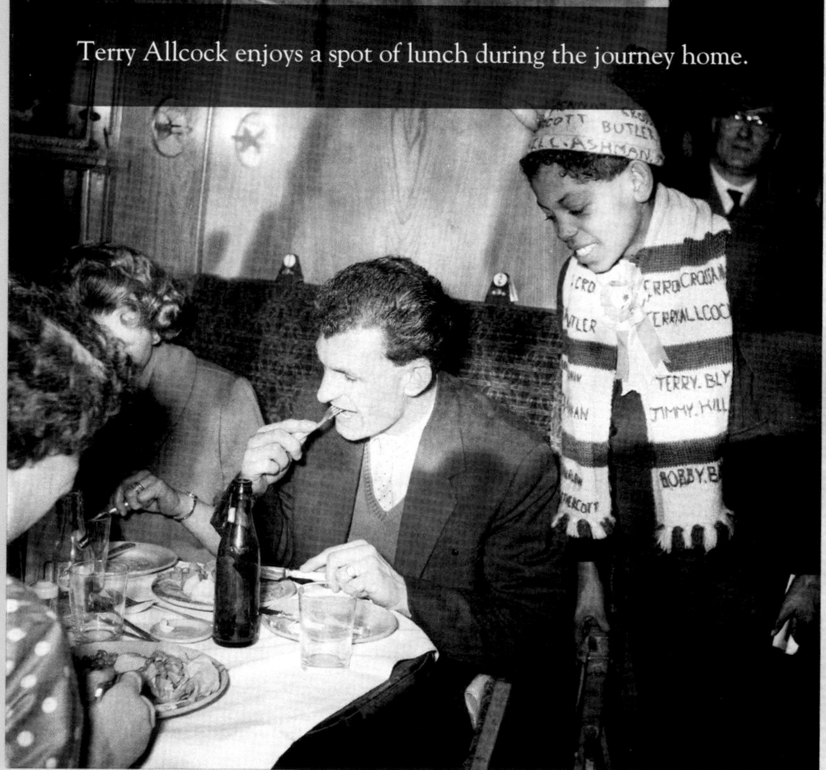

Terry Allcock enjoys a spot of lunch during the journey home.

On the Way to Division One

1959-1972

1971–72 team photo. Back row: Graham Paddon, Dave Stringer, Clive Payne, Duncan Forbes, Kevin Keelan, Mervyn Cawston, Steve Govier, Peter Silvester, Terry Anderson, Phil Hubbard. Front row: Ken Foggo, Geoff Butler, Doug Livermore, Max Briggs, Ron Saunders, Alan Black, Jimmy Bone, Trevor Howard, David Cross.

Promotion Again

Teams who go on unexpected cup runs often suffer a sense of deflation afterwards, but in 1959–60 manager Archie Macaulay was determined to mount a promotion challenge. The new South Stand (named after Mr (later Sir) Arthur South, who had helped rescue the club from financial ruin only two years earlier) was built, and big crowds packed Carrow Road throughout the season. There was no repeat of the glorious cup run (City went out in the first round) but this may have proved a blessing. Teams gunning for promotion need no distractions. Promotion was sealed on 27th April after a 4-3 home win against Southend United, during which there was almost a constant chorus of 'On the Ball, City'. In the end the club finished second in what was to be their last season in Division Three for 50 years. At the end of the season Terry Bly departed for Peterborough to the consternation of many City fans. He went on to score 52 goals in Peterborough's first season in the Football League.

Season Stats 1959–60

Ron Ashman **(46 appearances)**
Barry Butler **(46 appearances)**
Roy McCrohan **(46 appearances)**
Bryan Thurlow **(46 appearances)**
Matt Crowe **(45 appearances)**
Sandy Kennon **(45 appearances)**
Terry Allcock **(44 appearances)**
Errol Crossan **(43 appearances)**
Jimmy Hill **(38 appearances)**
Bill Punton **(27 appearances)**
Terry Bly **(25 appearances)**
Bobby Brennan **(20 appearances)**
Brian Whitehouse **(10 appearances)**
Bunny Larkin **(9 appearances)**
James Moran **(6 appearances)**
John Richards **(5 appearances)**
Ray Savino **(2 appearances)**
Bob Edwards **(1 appearance)**
Joe Mullett **(1 appearance)**
Brian Ronson **(1 appearance)**

Record: P46 W24 D11 L11 F82 A54 PTS59
Goals: Hill 16, Allcock 16, Crossan 13, Bly 7, Moran 5, Whitehouse 4, Brennan 4, Punton 4, Crowe 4, Larkin 3, Richards 2, Ashman 2, McCrohan 1, Butler 1
Manager: Archie Macaulay

The Canaries celebrate their promotion in the changing room.

LEFT: 4th February 1961, Norwich 4 Lincoln 1. Ron Ashman shakes hands with the Lincoln captain prior to the game.

BELOW: 16th September 1961, Norwich 3 Sunderland 1. Here Norwich's Bill Punton races to gain possession of the ball ahead of Sunderland's Colin Nelson.

-LEGENDS-

Tommy Bryceland

Scotsman Tommy Bryceland originally made his name playing for St Mirren FC; as an attacking midfielder he scored 47 goals in just 105 games and helped win them the Scottish Cup final. Bryceland joined Norwich in 1962, playing a big part in keeping Norwich City in Division Two and helping them achieve sixth place in 1965. In his final match for Norwich against Huddersfield on the 8th November 1969 he netted the only City goal, taking his total to 55 goals in 284 appearances. In 2003, following a vote by Norwich City fans, Tommy Bryceland was added to the Norwich City FC Hall of Fame.

FOOTBALL -STATS-

Tommy Bryceland

Name: Thomas Bryceland

Born: Greenock, 1st March 1939

Position: Inside-right

Norwich City Playing Career: 1962–69

Club Appearances: 281

Goals: 55

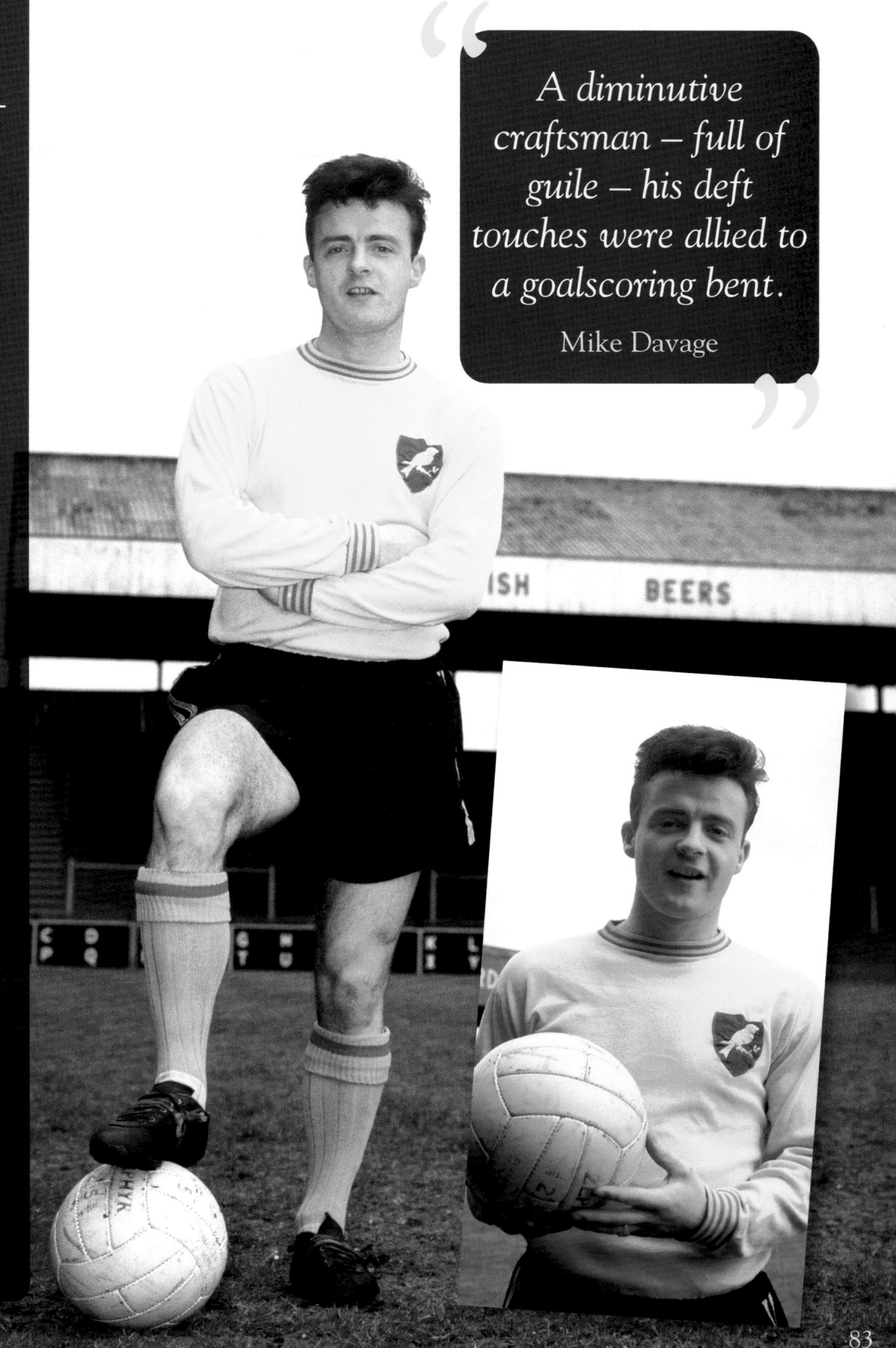

> *"A diminutive craftsman – full of guile – his deft touches were allied to a goalscoring bent."*
>
> Mike Davage

Teams who win promotion to Division Two often do well the following season, but Archie Macaulay and Ron Ashman were both keen to warn supporters not to be overly optimistic.

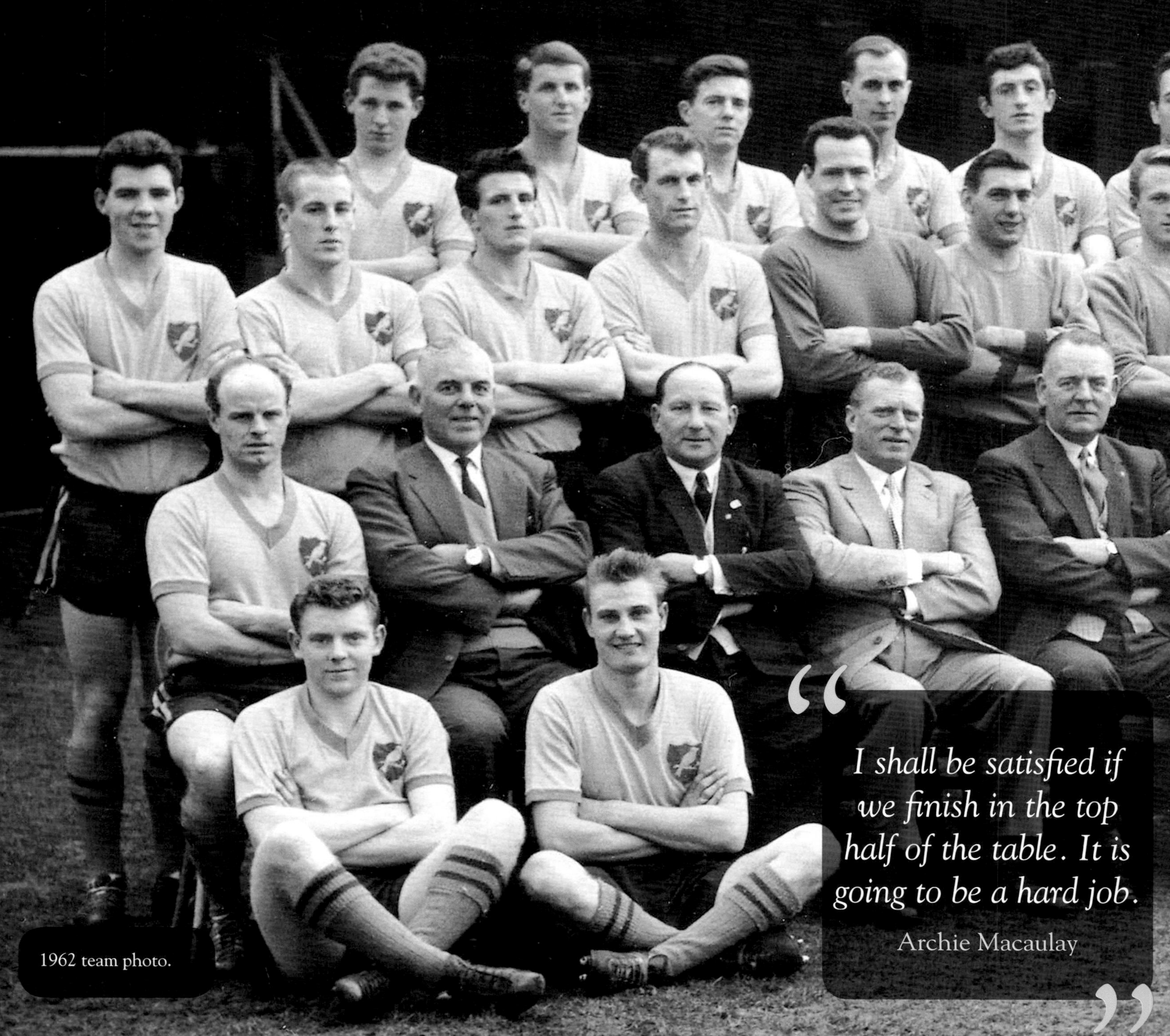

1962 team photo.

> *I shall be satisfied if we finish in the top half of the table. It is going to be a hard job.*
>
> Archie Macaulay

But their caution proved wrong-headed. Indeed, at one point it appeared both the Canaries and their local rivals Ipswich looked set for promotion. But it was not to be. Had a couple of new signings been made in the previous summer and had Terry Allcock not broken his leg in September (even though he still finished as the club's top scorer with 16 goals), things might have been different. In the end Norwich finished a very creditable fourth.

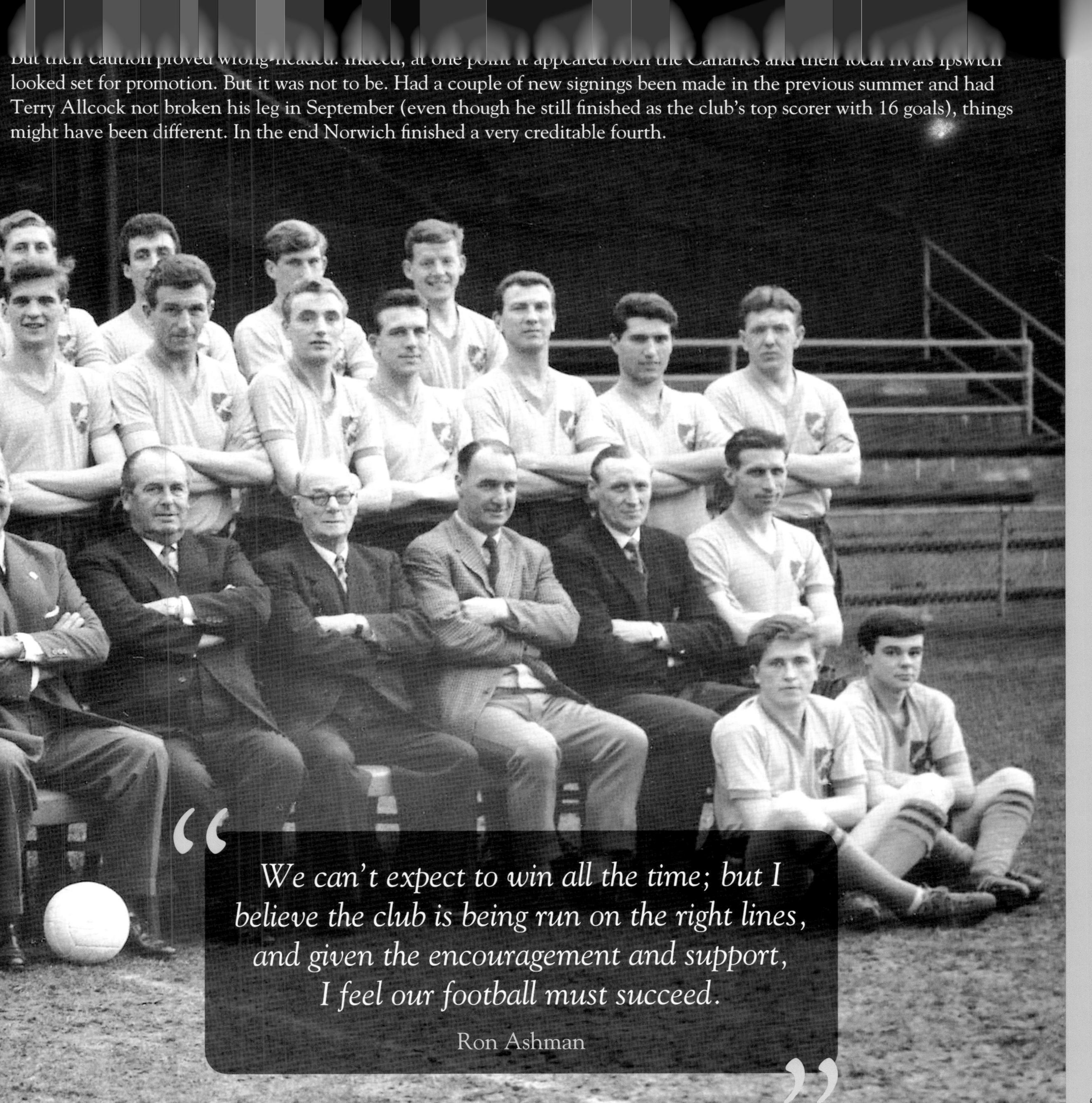

> *We can't expect to win all the time; but I believe the club is being run on the right lines, and given the encouragement and support, I feel our football must succeed.*
>
> Ron Ashman

League Cup Glory

In October 1961 Archie Macaulay stunned the club when he left to take over the reins at West Bromwich Albion. He was replaced by Willie Reid, the St Mirren manager.

The League Cup was in its infancy and many teams didn't take it very seriously, especially as there was no European qualification for the winners and the final didn't take place at Wembley. In only the second season of its existence, Norwich City unexpectedly reached the final. It's fair to say that their path to the final wasn't as testing as the 1959 FA Cup run, but, even so, it was an achievement of some note, as they despatched Chesterfield, Lincoln City, Middlesbrough, Sunderland and Blackpool along the way.

The final took place over two legs with fellow finalists Rochdale hosting the first leg, on 26th April 1962, at Spotland. Norwich won at a canter with Bill Punton and Derrick Lythgoe (2) scoring in a 3-0 win. The return leg was a formality, so much so that only 19,800 turned out to see Norwich win their first ever major cup trophy in a 1-0 win, courtesy of a Jimmy Hill goal. The Rochdale manager Tony Collins had played for Norwich, making 31 appearances between 1953 and 1955, and was the league's first black manager.

ABOVE: Willie Reid took over as City manager in December 1961.

League Cup 1961–62: The Road to Cup Glory

First Round	13th September	Chesterfield	A	3–2	Allcock, Hill, Savino
Second Round	4th October	Lincoln City	H	3–2	Allcock, Mannion, Scott
Third Round	15th November	Middlesbrough	H	3–2	Conway, Mannion, og
Fourth Round	7th February	Sunderland	A	4–1	McCrohan, Hill, Lythgoe, Burton
Semi-Final	11th April	Blackpool	H	4–1	Hill, Punton, Lythoe, Scott
	16th April	Blackpool	A	0–2	
Final	26th April	Rochdale	A	3–0	Punton, Lythgoe 2
	1st May	Rochdale	H	1–0	Hill

Perhaps the main achievement in 1962 was the FA Cup fourth-round triumph over Ipswich Town. Ipswich were flying high under Alf Ramsey and would go on to win the Division One championship, but they hadn't reckoned with being knocked out of the FA Cup by their East Anglian rivals. After a 1-1 draw at Carrow Road, Norwich travelled to Portman Road to win through two goals from the prolific Terry Allcock.

Fans queue for free tickets for the CCTV broadcast of the Norwich v Ipswich Town game on 27th January 1962.

BELOW: City goalkeeper Sandy Kennon is challenged by Ipswich's Ray Crawford. 27th January 1962, Norwich 1 Ipswich 1.

The Forward Five

The season was to end in a bizarre fashion. Willie Reid, who had been in the job less than five months, decided Norfolk was not for him, and despite winning a trophy returned north of the border. His successor, George Swindin, didn't even last that long, and left for Cardiff City in November 1962. The board decided to play safe and appoint team captain Ron Ashman to the post: it was his task to settle the club down and build for the future. He took the team to an 11th place finish, six higher than the previous season.

This picture captures the City forward line of the day, from 7 to 11 order. They are (left to right): Gerry Mannion, Terry Allcock, Jim Conway, Jimmy Hill and Derrick Lythgoe.

–LEGENDS–

Ron Ashman

Many Canaries fans would argue that Ron Ashman is the greatest player to don the famous yellow-and-green shirt. Ashman played for Norwich City for just over 16 years and then went on to manage the club that meant so much to him, earning the FA 20-year long service statuette. His total of 662 appearances has only been beaten by Kevin Keelan, the goalkeeper he signed as manager in July 1963. During his playing career he scored 56 goals, scoring in 11 successive seasons: a Norwich City record. Ashman was there during the 1957 crisis, he was a vital member of the 1959 cup run team, helped secure promotion in 1960 and was part of the team that got Norwich its first trophy in 1962. He may have gone, but he will never be forgotten.

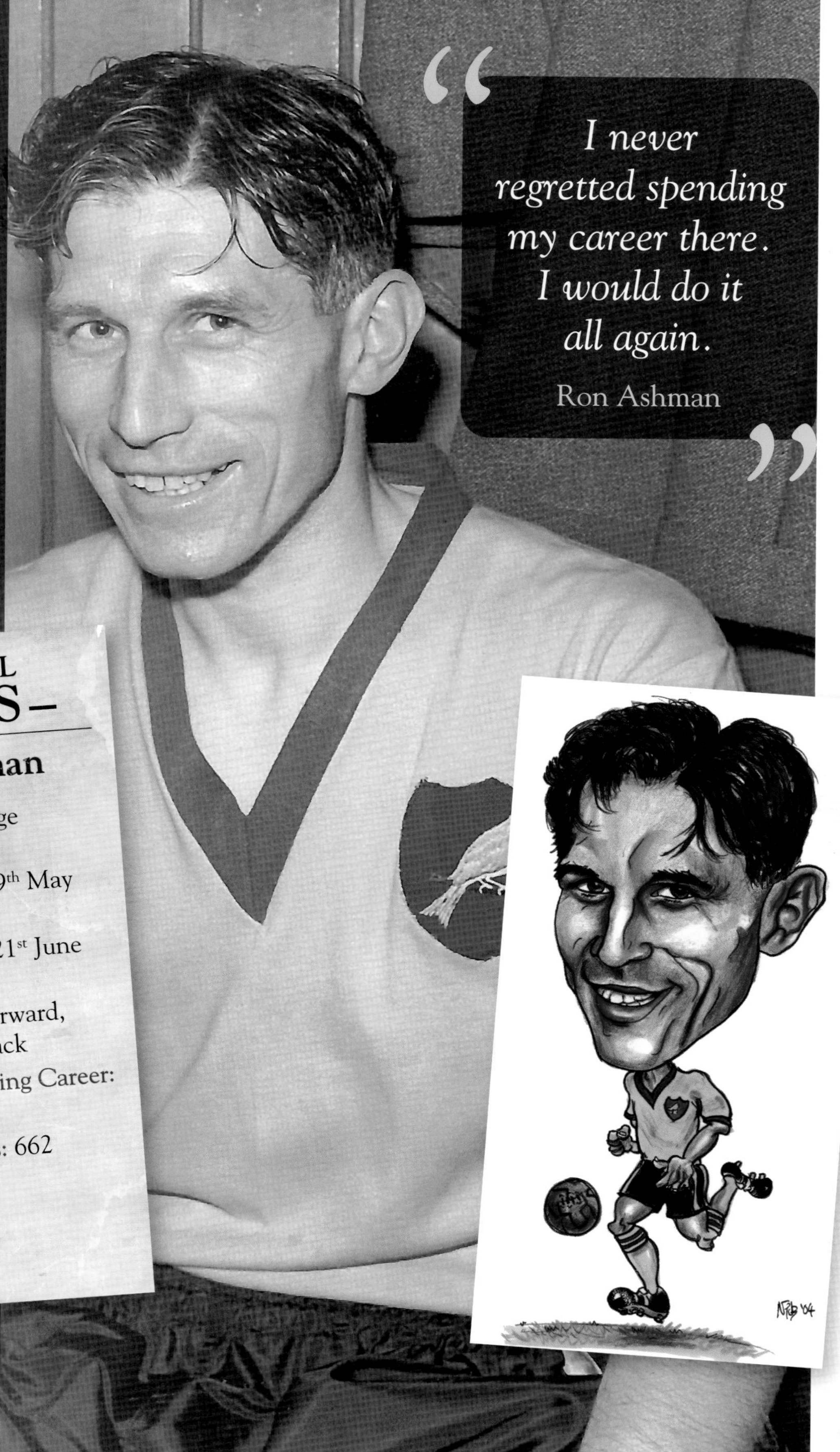

FOOTBALL –STATS–

Ron Ashman

Name: Ronald George Ashman

Born: Whittlesey, 19th May 1926

Died: Scunthorpe, 21st June 2004

Position: Centre-forward, left-half and full-back

Norwich City Playing Career: 1947–63

Club Appearances: 662

Goals: 56

> *"I never regretted spending my career there. I would do it all again."*
>
> Ron Ashman

Five significant things happened in 1963. Terry Allcock piled in four goals in a 5-0 FA Cup trouncing of Newcastle United, and in the next (sixth) round a record 43,984 crowd watched the Canaries crash out 2-0 to Leicester City. In July, a young goalkeeper by the name of Kevin Keelan was signed from Wrexham. He would go on to be a Norwich City legend, playing 673 games. In addition, in September striker Ron Davies was signed from Luton Town, having scored four goals against Norwich back in April.

Davies proved an instant hit, scoring in his first four games and bagging 30 overall in his first season. The fifth and final significant happening of 1963 was the fact that Ron Ashman played his 590th and final league game for the club. Having been acting player-manager, he was duly appointed to the manager's job full-time. But the club was still in transition and finished the season in a lowly 17th place after a respectable 11th place finish in 1962–63.

> *"If he fails his medical, then sack the doctor."*
>
> Geoffrey Watling on the signing of Ron Davies

30th March 1963, Norwich 0 Leicester 2. Leicester's Gordon Banks punches a shot from Terry Allcock. Note the fans are standing in front of the perimeter fence due to a record crowd of 43,984.

Norwich's Terry Allcock and Jimmy Hill find themselves outnumbered by Leicester defenders.

Goalkeeper Sandy Kennon up against Leicester's goalscorer Dave Gibson.

The Two Rons

ABOVE: The 1963–64 team. Back row (left to right): Terry Allcock, Gerry Mannion, Ken Hill, Sandy Kennon, Barry Butler, Kevin Keelan, Fred Sharpe, Joe Mullett, Bill Punton. Front row: Billy Furness, Phil Kelly, Tommy Bryceland, Mike Sutton, Ron Ashman (manager), Jim Oliver, Ron Barnes, Ron Davies, George Lee (trainer). Seated in front: Colin Worrell and Jackie Bell.

RIGHT: Ron Ashman prior to the Blackburn Rovers game on 5th March 1966.

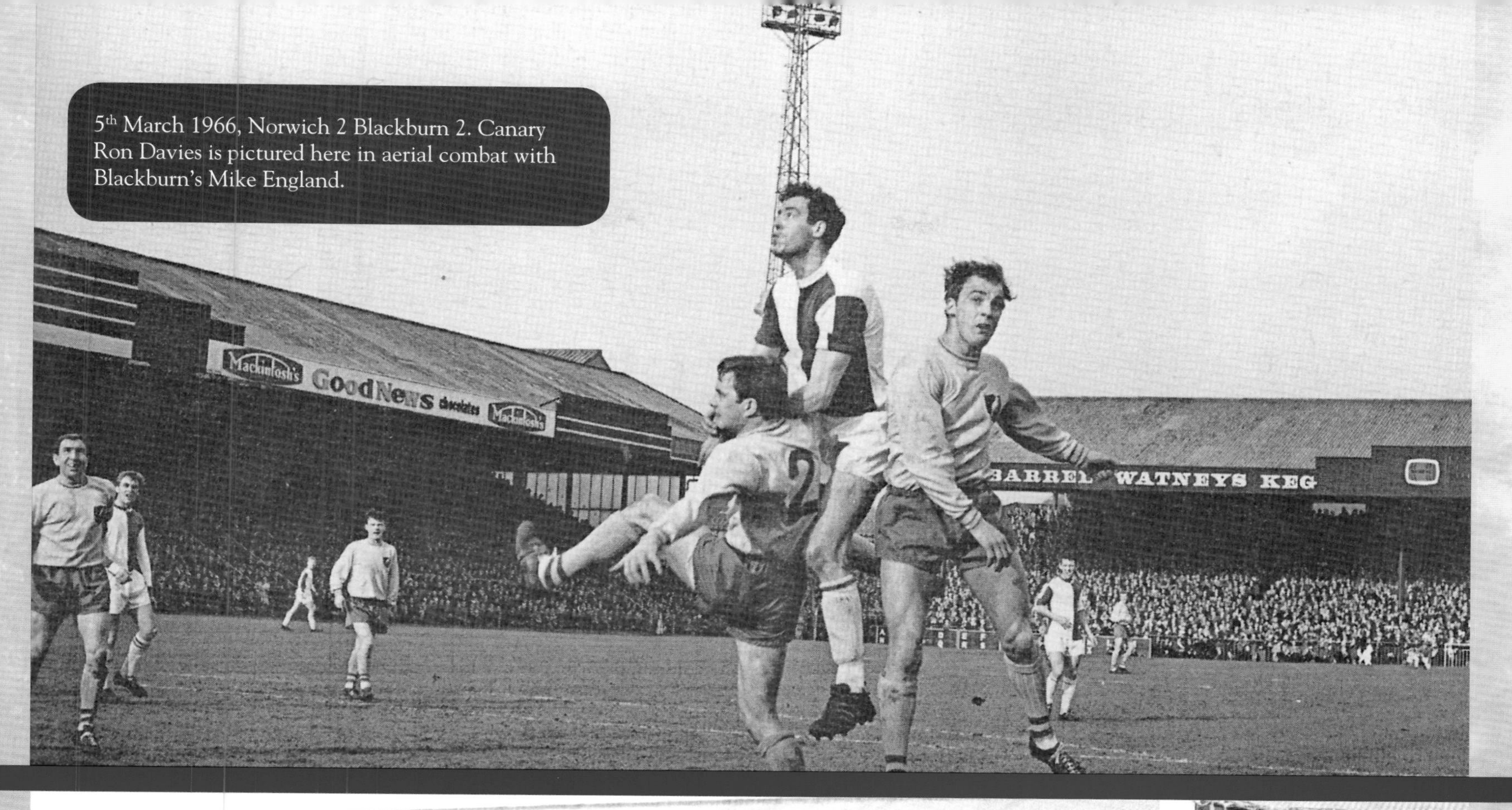

5th March 1966, Norwich 2 Blackburn 2. Canary Ron Davies is pictured here in aerial combat with Blackburn's Mike England.

A crowd of 30,751 watched this goal by Norwich's Ron Davies; Blackburn's goalkeeper Fred Else is powerless to stop it.

The 1965–66 season failed to match the hopes of the previous season's sixth place finish. It was a season tinged with tragedy and disappointment. The tragedy came when popular defender Barry Butler was killed in a road accident. In a tribute to Butler, the board decided to hold a Player of the Year competition, which they named the Barry Butler Memorial Trophy, in commemoration of him.

BELOW: The Canaries celebrate with their manager Ron Ashman, after their 2-2 draw with Blackburn on 5th March.

–LEGENDS– Barry Butler

Barry Butler is a true Norwich City legend: not only did he play for City for nine years but he showed extraordinary talent and must be regarded as one of the club's greatest ever centre-halves. As captain he led by example and overcame many obstacles including a broken leg, a fractured cheekbone and wrist, and even pneumonia. He came to Norwich from Sheffield Wednesday in 1957 and went on to make 349 appearances. Sadly, on 9th April 1966, his football career came to an abrupt end as he was tragically killed in a car accident. After his death the board decided to name their Player of the Year award "The Barry Butler Memorial Trophy" in honour of his dedication to the club.

FOOTBALL –STATS–

Barry Butler

Name: Barry Butler
Born: Stockton-on-Tees, 30th July 1934
Died: Norwich, 9th April 1966
Position: Centre-half
Norwich City Playing Career: 1957–66
Club Appearances: 349
Goals: 3

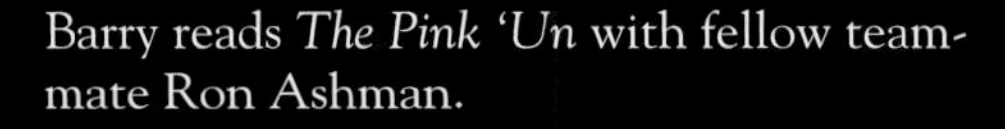

Barry reads *The Pink 'Un* with fellow team-mate Ron Ashman.

> *"Everyone respected Barry. He was one of the finest players that ever turned out for the Canaries."*
>
> Ted Bell

RIP Barry Butler

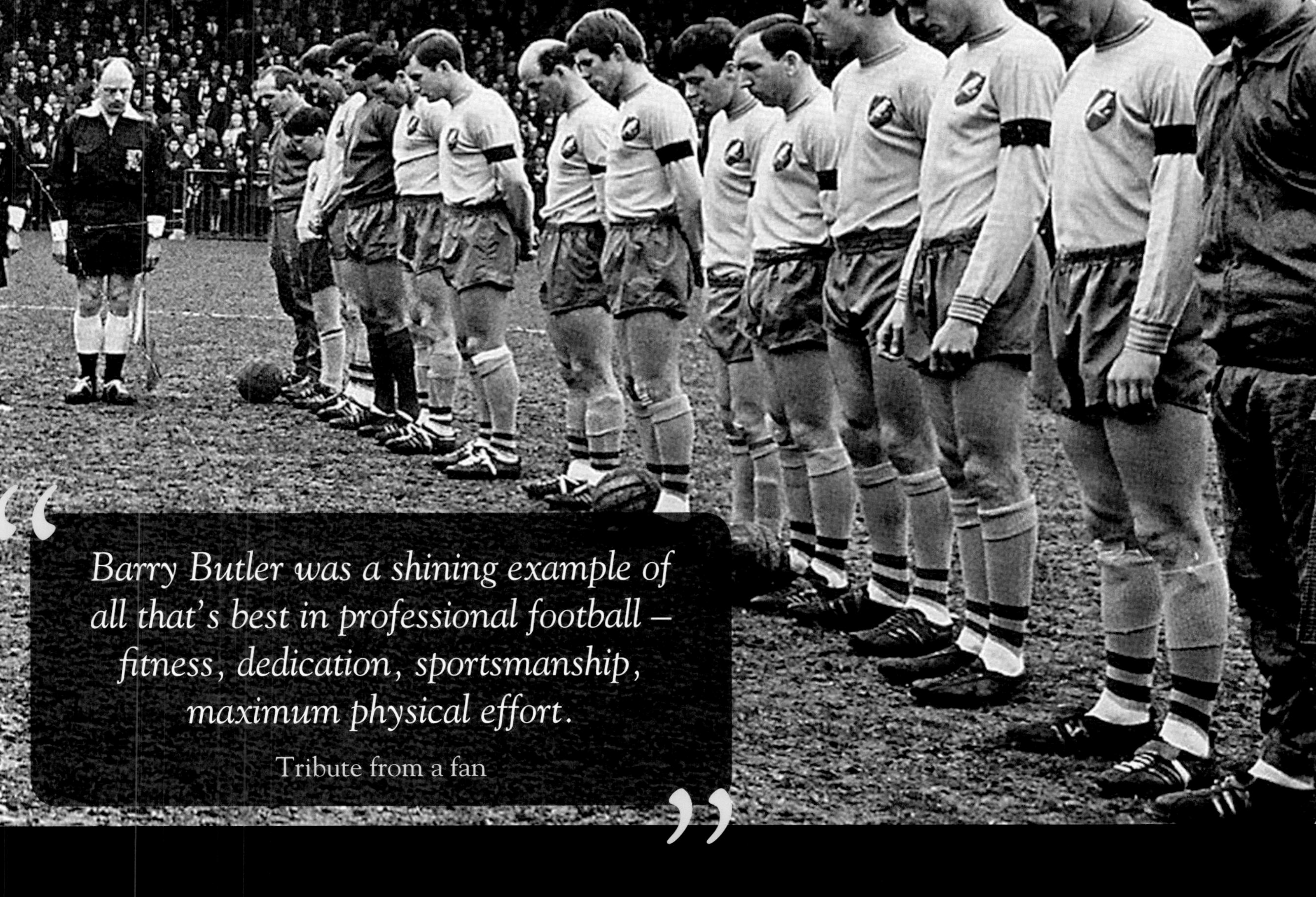

Barry Butler was a shining example of all that's best in professional football – fitness, dedication, sportsmanship, maximum physical effort.

Tribute from a fan

Carrow Road paid tribute to Barry Butler with a minute's silence before a home game against Rotherham United on Monday 11th April 1966.

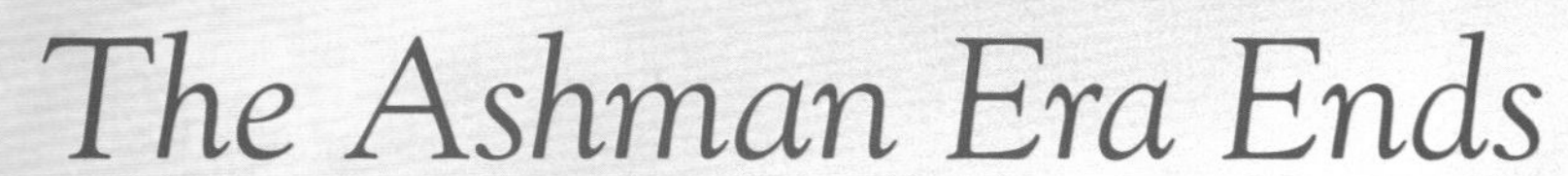

The Ashman Era Ends

A 13th place finish at the end of 1965–66 season was enough for the board to want to make a change and Ron Ashman's services were dispensed with. It was a brutal way for a 20-year relationship to end.

New manager Lol Morgan, who joined from Darlington, lost little time in reshaping the team, signing a whole host of new players. But fans were devastated and uncomprehending when the club decided to sell top goalscorer Ron Davies to Southampton for a bargain £60,000. Although the goals had dried up a little, he was still at the top of his game, as evidenced by the 134 goals he proceeded to score in 240 games on the south coast.

> *I went into the job with my eyes wide open, knowing what would happen if we did not get results. Consequently, like many more managers, I have fallen by the wayside.*
>
> Ron Ashman, on his dismissal

ABOVE: Lol Morgan hard at work.

–LEGENDS–

Terry Allcock

Terry Allcock, known as "The Count" by fans, is City's second greatest goalscorer with 127 goals to his name, just five goals behind Johnny Gavin. Although he spent most of his career as a forward, in his last five seasons he was a half-back, something which undoubtedly stopped him from becoming the top goalscorer. He joined Norwich City from Bolton Wanderers in 1958, and made his debut against Millwall on 15th March of that year. He was a crucial goalscorer in the 1959 cup run, and despite breaking his leg in 1960 he was back on the pitch in 100 days. Allcock went on to play for 11 years in total, leaving fans devastated when he retired in 1969. Allcock is still a regular at Carrow Road and can often be seen entertaining the Club's guests with his stories of 1959.

FOOTBALL –STATS–

Terry Allcock

Name: Terence Allcock

Born: Leeds, 10th December 1935

Position: Forward and half-back

Norwich City Playing Career: 1958–69

Club Appearances: 389

Goals: 127

The highlight of Lol Morgan's first season in charge came in the FA Cup when, having dumped Derby County out of the FA Cup in the third round, City went to Old Trafford in the fourth and beat high-flying Manchester United 2-1 – Best, Charlton and Law to boot. Unfortunately the glory was short-lived as the Canaries went down 3-1 to Sheffield Wednesday in the sixth round.

ABOVE: Laurie Brown hammers the ball clear during a Manchester United attack in the FA Cup fourth round on 18th February 1967.

ABOVE: Laurie Brown heads off another challenge from United.

ABOVE: United's Nobby Stiles looks on in horror as Gordon Bolland takes the ball and is about to knock in the winning goal.

ABOVE: A 63,405 strong crowd watched as Gordon Bolland scored the winning goal, resulting in the shock win for Norwich.

Don Heath and Gordon Bolland celebrate their goals in the changing room.

ABOVE: Hugh Curran heads in Norwich's third and final goal in a 4-3 defeat at home to Ipswich, 3rd February 1968.

Another Managerial Departure

Lol Morgan never proved popular with the crowd and to be honest had had little success on the pitch. Finishes of 11th and ninth were nothing to write home about. He wasn't really given time to build the team he wanted, but there's little doubt that he sowed the seeds for the success achieved in later years. Under his tenure David Stringer became a regular and Duncan Forbes was signed – two legends who personified Norwich City throughout the next decade. By the end of the 1968–69 season the board had become frustrated and in April they sacked Lol Morgan. When asked if it had come as a surprise, the ex-Norwich manager said "no".

BELOW: Norwich 3 Ipswich 4.

Alan Black heads clear during a Chelsea attack. Chelsea 1 Norwich 0.

December 1968. Back row (left to right): Ken Foggo, Trevor Howard, Gerry Howshall, Dave Stringer, Kevin Keelan, Terry Anderson, Geoff Butler. Front row: Neil O'Donnell, John Manning, Ken Mallender, Hugh Curran, Duncan Forbes.

–LEGENDS–

Dave Stringer

Dave Stringer is remembered fondly as a player and a manager; he remained loyal to the Canaries and is third place in the Norwich City All-Time Appearances table, playing 499 games for City. Stringer and Duncan Forbes were a class act and were instrumental in City's success in the 1970s. Stringer returned to the Canaries in 1984 to manage the youth side, and would continue to rise up the managerial ranks until eventually, in 1987, he was appointed manager after the sacking of Ken Brown. As manager he oversaw one of the most successful season Norwich City ever had – the 1988–89 season – which featured Norwich in the league title race, topping the league at several stages before finishing fourth, and also reaching the semi-finals of the FA Cup. Stringer also signed some legendary Canary heroes such as Tim Sherwood and Robert Fleck, before eventually resigning in 1992.

RIGHT: Dave Stringer being presented with the Barry Butler Memorial Trophy by Geoffrey Watling.

FOOTBALL –STATS–

Dave Stringer

Name: David Ronald Stringer

Born: Great Yarmouth, 15th October 1944

Position: Defender

Norwich City Playing Career: 1965–76

Club Appearances: 499

Goals: 22

Enter Ron Saunders

The appointment of Ron Saunders as manager in July 1969 proved to be the trigger that eventually shot Norwich into the big time. As a player, Saunders had scored more than 200 league goals, and following his retirement in 1967 he spent two years as manager of Southern League Yeovil, before a short stint at Oxford United. Saunders knew he would have no money to spend at Norwich and would have to inspire his players to greater things.

Saunders quickly gained a reputation as a tough disciplinarian and a man who would push his players to the limits. Because of the continuing financial tightrope the club was walking, Ron Saunders had precious few funds to use to bring new players in. Peter Silvester signed from Reading for £20,000 and finished the season with 10 goals, while tough-tackling midfielder Graham Paddon came from Coventry for £25,000. He became one of the club's most popular players during his two spells with the club. There were murmurings about negative tactics but supporters could see that, gradually, results were coming. However, Saunders' first season in charge was unspectacular and resulted in an 11th place finish, although it did include an end-of-season 6-0 trouncing of Birmingham.

The 1970–71 season proved little more successful than the previous one and the club finished 10th, but the more intelligent supporters already detected signs of a growing defensive prowess, which would be vital if Norwich were to push for promotion the next season. But it was the signing of Doug Livermore from Liverpool which gave the Canaries' midfield a strength it had been lacking and would be vital in the promotion campaign.

LEFT: Ron Saunders hard at work.

RIGHT: Ron Saunders, Norwich City manager.

> *We weren't prepared to take 'no' for an answer. We feel that this young man has all the capabilities required and that with any luck at all he can be a great asset to this club.*
>
> Chairman Geoffrey Watling on his new manager

ABOVE: 12th February 1972, Norwich 2 Millwall 2. Norwich's Doug Livermore has the ball, watched on the right by Graham Paddon.

BELOW: 25th March 1972, Norwich 5 Blackpool 1. Pictured is Duncan Forbes clearing a Blackpool attack.

Winning Promotion

The 1971–72 season started well, following a successful pre-season tour of Portugal. Norwich were top by the end of September. Indeed, they only suffered a single defeat in the first half of the season, a remarkable record. Goals had proved hard to come by in previous seasons but the signings of the imposing centre-forward David Cross from Rochdale and the fiery Jimmy Bone provided the attacking prowess which had been lacking. Although not a prolific scorer (he bagged eight during the season), Cross led the City line with strength and determination. A blow was suffered when captain Duncan Forbes tore a hamstring at the end of October and was ruled out until March, but even this could not thwart the club's onward march. Millwall were their nearest challengers and in mid-February the two clubs met at Carrow Road in an exciting 2-2 draw, watched by nearly 34,000.

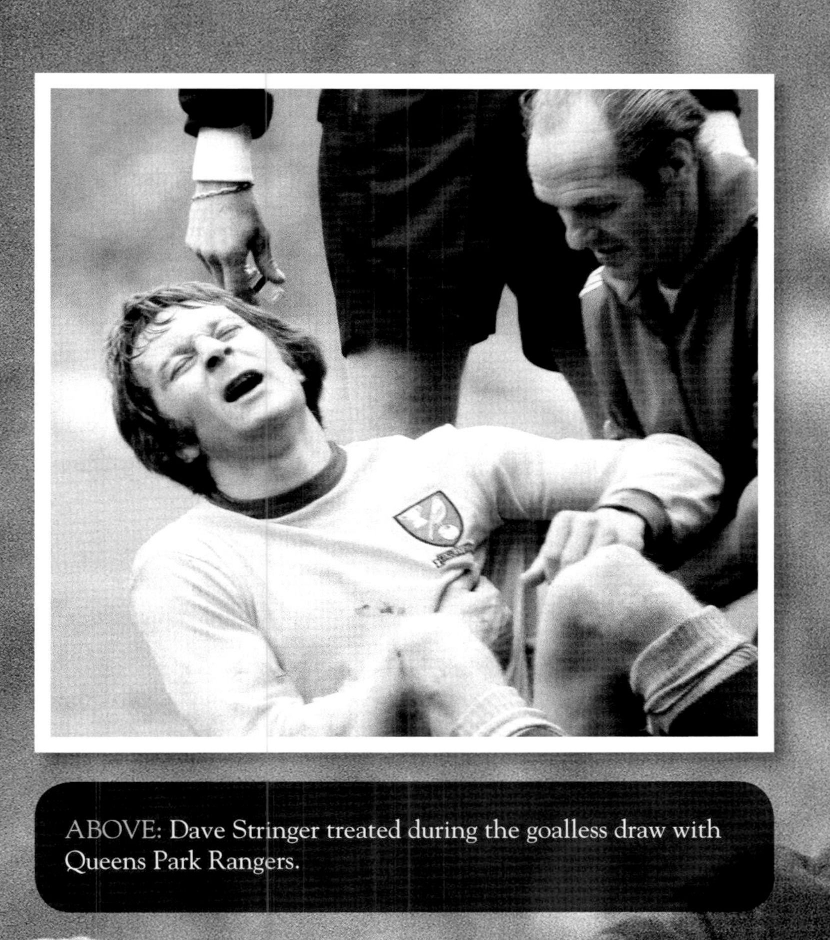

ABOVE: Dave Stringer treated during the goalless draw with Queens Park Rangers.

ALL PHOTOS: 3rd April 1972, Queens Park Rangers 0 Norwich 0.

A fortnight later a 4-0 defeat at Birmingham saw Norwich knocked off the top spot for the first time in nearly six months. But this was a temporary setback. The Canaries clinched promotion on 24th April when they travelled to Orient and beat the O's 2-1, with Ken Foggo and Graham Paddon notching the goals. It had taken 70 years for Norwich City to reach Division One and they had done it in style. The following week a goal from David Stringer clinched both a 1-1 draw at Watford and the Division Two championship.

BELOW: 24th April 1972, Leyton Orient 1 Norwich 2.

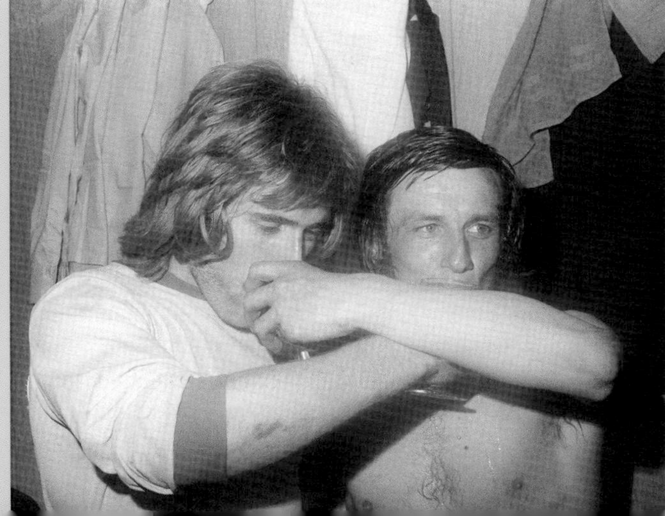

ABOVE: David Cross celebrates after Ken Foggo had just put City ahead.

LEFT: Goalscorers Graham Paddon and Ken Foggo celebrate with some champagne.

29th April 1972, Watford 1 Norwich 1. Dave Stringer scores the goal against Watford which results in the Canaries clinching the Division Two championship.

TELEGRAM

RECEIVED

Prefix. Time handed in. Office of Origin and Service Instructions. Words.

At

To

By

G6 N236 19.30 BUCKINGHAM PALACE 51

LORD MAYOR OF NORWICH CITY HALL NORWICH

= I AM DELIGHTED THAT NORWICH HAVE TODAY BECOME CHAMPIONS OF THE SECOND DIVISION . PLEASE CONVEY MY WARMEST CONGRATULATIONS TO THEIR MANAGER AND TO ALL MEMBERS OF THE TEAM AND MY BEST WISHES FOR NEXT SEASON IN THE FIRST DIVISION = ELIZABETH R QUEEN MOTHER

BELOW: Stringer celebrates his goal with Max Briggs and Jimmy Bone.

ABOVE: This telegram was sent immediately from Buckingham Palace after Norwich won the title of Division Two champions.

1971–72
Champions Division Two

Players

Kevin Keelan **(42 appearances)**
Clive Payne **(42 appearances)**
Dave Stringer **(42 appearances)**
Doug Livermore **(41 appearances)**
Ken Foggo **(40 appearances)**
Graham Paddon **(40 appearances)**
Terry Anderson **(34 appearances)**
David Cross **(32 appearances)**
Max Briggs **(27 appearances)**
Duncan Forbes **(27 appearances)**
Peter Silvester **(26 appearances)**
Geoff Butler **(23 appearances)**
Alan Black **(20 appearances)**
Trevor Howard **(20 appearances)**
Jimmy Bone **(13 appearances)**
Phil Hubbard **(8 appearances)**
Malcolm Darling **(4 appearances)**
Bobby Bell **(3 appearances)**
Steve Govier **(3 appearances)**
Neil O'Donnell **(2 appearances)**
Steve Grapes **(1 appearance)**
Gary Sargent **(1 appearance)**

Record: P42 W21 D15 L6 F60 A36 PTS57
Goals: Foggo 13, Silvester 12, Cross 8, Paddon 8, Howard 5, Bone 4, Stringer 4, Forbes 2, Govier 1, Darling 1, Hubbard 1, own goal 1
Manager: Ron Saunders

ABOVE: This is a picture of the championship-winning squad recording their own disc *The Canaries* at the Norwood Rooms in May 1972.

BELOW: Division Two champions travelling in style.

LEFT: 1971–72 champions.

"At times I took a lot of stick for being aggressive, but I wouldn't let those people down [Norwich fans], and I did some silly things in my time. There was a fella by the name of Robson who played for Northampton. He kept on at me when I caught the ball, so I tucked it under one arm and just punched him with the other.

Norwich City goalkeeping legend Kevin Keelan talking to the BBC, prior to a return visit to Carrow Road in May 2008, about the way he played the game"

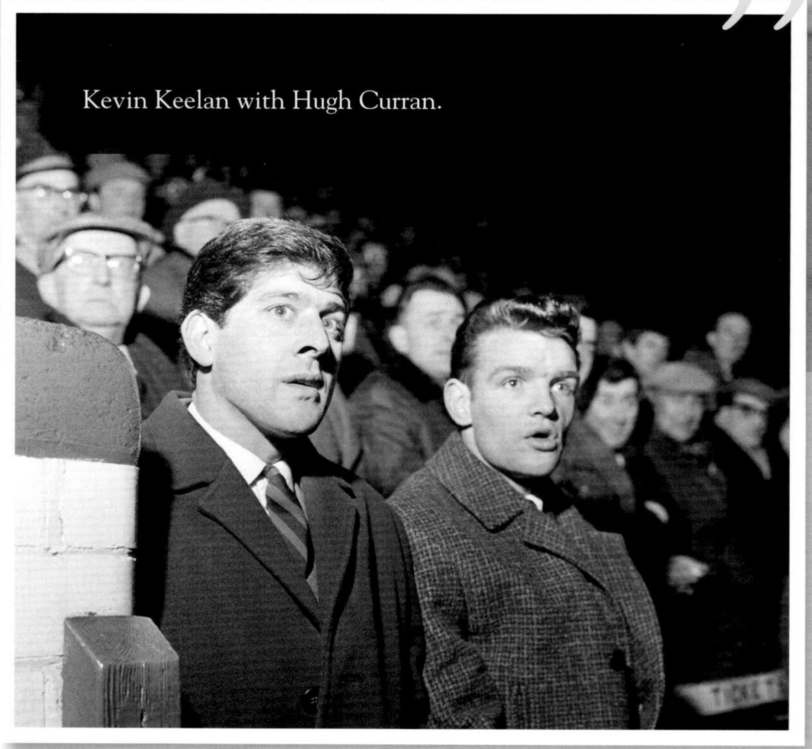

Kevin Keelan with Hugh Curran.

Celebrating with Doug Livermore, Jimmy Bone and David Cross.

-LEGENDS-

Kevin Keelan MBE

Kevin Keelan is one of Norwich City's most recognizable faces and recently topped a poll of *Evening News* readers as the ultimate Norwich City FC legend, with nearly double the amount of votes of the next placed. After stints at Aston Villa, Stockport and Wrexham, he moved to Norwich in 1963 for £6,500 in what Ron Ashman would later describe as "the bargain of the century". Keelan made a grand total of 673 appearances for City, making him the record holder as the Canary with the most appearances, something which is unlikely to be beaten in the modern game. His career, spanning 17 years, included Norwich City's promotion to Division One in 1972 and subsequent relegation; it also included two League Cup finals at Wembley in 1973 and 1975, and he went down in history as the first goalkeeper ever to save a penalty at Wembley when he stopped Ray Graydon's spot kick. Keelan's final game was on 9th February 1980, in an amazing match which saw the Canaries defeated by Liverpool 5-3. During his career he was honoured with the Player of the Year on two occasions, and in 2002 was made an inaugural member of the Norwich City FC Hall of Fame.

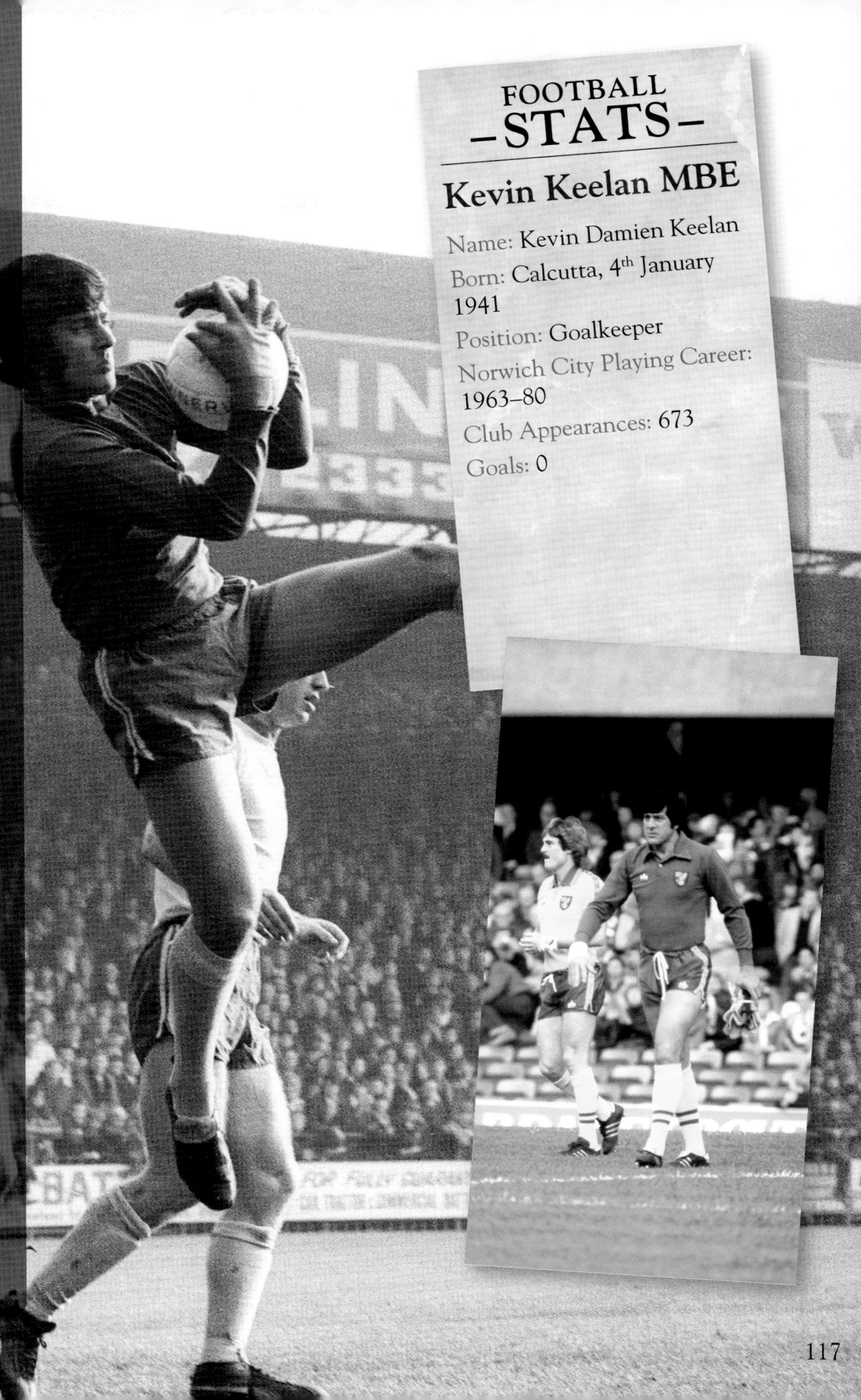

FOOTBALL
-STATS-

Kevin Keelan MBE

Name: Kevin Damien Keelan
Born: Calcutta, 4th January 1941
Position: Goalkeeper
Norwich City Playing Career: 1963–80
Club Appearances: 673
Goals: 0

Ups and Downs 1972-1985

Norwich City FC in London for the League Cup final against Aston Villa, showing off their green suits for their arrival at Wembley, 26th February 1975.

Playing with the Big Boys

The summer of 1972 was a busy one, as the club prepared to play in Division One for the first time in their history. The big day soon arrived and on Saturday 12th August Everton came to Carrow Road. The game ended 1-1, with the Norwich goal scored by Jimmy Bone. A few days later the Canaries travelled to Ipswich where two goals from Jimmy Bone and Terry Anderson enabled Norwich to beat their chief rivals 2-1. Further victories over leading sides saw the Canaries rising to dizzy heights. Perhaps the highlight of the season came just before Christmas when Norwich travelled to Highbury and beat Arsenal 3-0, with a hat-trick from the ever impressive Graham Paddon. But this kind of form was not to last.

A run of 19 games without a win saw them plummet into the relegation zone. It wasn't until April 1973 that the tide turned and three wins against Chelsea, West Bromwich Albion and Crystal Palace saw the club stave off relegation by a whisker. Although no new players had been signed prior to the start of the season, Ron Saunders brought in Colin Suggett, Trevor Hockey and Ian Mellor, while shipping out the long-serving Ken Foggo to Portsmouth and the much-admired Jimmy Bone to Sheffield United. Norwich still enjoy the distinction of being the last club to finish third from bottom of the top division and not be relegated; three up, three down was only introduced the following season.

ABOVE: Graham Paddon celebrates his goal against Leicester City. 21st October 1972, Norwich City 2 Leicester City 1.

ABOVE: Duncan Forbes leads out the Canaries for their first ever game in Division One, against Everton on Saturday 12th August.

Jimmy Bone scores Norwich City's first ever Division One goal against Everton. The game ended 1-1.

28th October 1972, Norwich City 1 Liverpool 1.

Abandoned!

ALL PHOTOS: 13th December 1972, Chelsea 0 Norwich 2. Norwich overcame Chelsea with goals from Jimmy Bone and David Cross. The return leg at Carrow Road had to be abandoned due to fog, with Norwich leading 3-2. In the rematch, Norwich won 1-0 through a Steve Govier goal.

Wembley Beckons

The 1972–73 season was also memorable due to the fact that Norwich fought their way through to two cup finals. In the Texaco Cup they met local rivals Ipswich, but lost both games of the two-legged final 2-1.

They also reached the League Cup final for the second time, but this time it was rather more glorious as the tie was played at Wembley.

In the semi-final Norwich triumphed over Chelsea, albeit only after the second leg had to be replayed due to the original match being abandoned, with only five minutes remaining, when Norwich were 3-2 up. The first leg at Stamford Bridge resulted in a 2-0 win for Norwich. In the replay of the second leg they won 1-0 to reach the final against Tottenham Hotspur on 3rd March. It proved to be a disappointing day for the thousands of travelling Canaries fans who trekked down the A11 and round the North Circular. The match itself was a let-down and Spurs won 1-0 through a goal from Ralph Coates.

ABOVE: Jim Blair and Kevin Keelan travel in the team's luxury coach to Wembley.

BELOW: City chairman Geoffrey Watling (right) displays this Wembley cake he had baked specially for the after-match banquet.

The two teams, led by their managers Ron Saunders and Bill Nicholson, enter the pitch before the League Cup final at Wembley Stadium, 3rd March 1973. Tottenham Hotspur 1 Norwich City 0.

Final captains Duncan Forbes and Martin Peters meet the officials.

Jim Blair on the ball.

Graham Paddon pursued by a trio of Spurs players.

Wembley Defeat

RIGHT: David Cross and Jim Blair in full flow.

BELOW: Clive Payne running with the ball.

–LEGENDS–

Duncan Forbes

Duncan Forbes is without a doubt one of the most loyal and dedicated Canaries, spending 32 unbroken years at Carrow Road, 12 as a player, seven as part of the commercial staff and a further 13 as chief scout until his retirement in 2001. Forbes moved from Colchester United to Norwich City in 1968 for £10,000, and would go on to make 357 appearances for City till his retirement from the game in 1980. During his time at City, Forbes formed an amazing partnership with Dave Stringer and led City to two promotions and two cup finals as captain. Forbes is one of the inaugural members of the Norwich City FC Hall of Fame.

FOOTBALL –STATS–

Duncan Forbes

Name: Duncan Scott Forbes
Born: Edinburgh, 19th June 1941
Position: Centre-half
Norwich City Playing Career: 1968–80
Club Appearances: 357
Goals: 12

-LEGENDS-

Graham Paddon

Graham Paddon came to Norwich City from Coventry City in 1969 for £25,000 and was pivotal in the 1971–72 promotion team and the 1972–73 League Cup side. However, he was sold to West Ham in 1973 for the princely sum of £170,000. He remained at West Ham for three years and was part of the team that won the 1975 FA Cup final, but in 1976 he was brought back to Carrow Road for £110,000. During the third game of his return Paddon broke his leg and, although he recovered, many fans thought he had lost his previous sparkle. Despite this, in his second spell at Norwich, Paddon made more than 100 appearances, taking his grand total for City to 340 appearances.

FOOTBALL -STATS-

Graham Paddon

Name: Graham Charles Paddon

Born: Manchester, 24th August 1950

Died: Norfolk, 19th November 2007

Position: Forward

Norwich City Playing Career: 1969–73, 1976–81

Club Appearances: 340

Goals: 37

Sometimes as his captain I had to have a little word with him, about something or other, but whereas some players might answer you back, Graham didn't, he just did what was asked of him. He was such a lovely lad, quietly spoken – just a real nice guy and a real good footballer.

Duncan Forbes on the late, great Graham Paddon

Farewell Ron Saunders

City's second season in Division One was not a happy one either on the playing field or in the boardroom. Long-serving chairman Geoffrey Watling resigned, and at the end of August was succeeded by civic leader Arthur South, who had been instrumental in saving the club in financial ruin back in 1957. A run of only two wins in the first 16 matches saw rising discontent with Ron Saunders and his playing style. This culminated in a major falling-out with the board, following a 3-1 home defeat to Everton. The result? The resignation of Ron Saunders. The whole city was stunned. The man who had led the Canaries to two cup finals and the Division Two championship was gone. His successor could not have been more different. If Saunders was a dour disciplinarian, John Bond was just the opposite – ebullient, stylish and a show-off. Sadly, Bond couldn't prevent relegation at the end of the season despite a number of shrewd buys in the transfer market. Even semi-final appearances in the League and Texaco Cups couldn't mask the fact that it had been a dire season for the club. But, ever the optimist, John Bond promised great times ahead.

7th May 1973, Ipswich Town 2 Norwich City 1. Texaco Cup final Second Leg. Ipswich won 4-2 on aggregate. Ipswich's Eric Gates with the shot.

ABOVE: 25th August 1973, Wolves 3 Norwich City 1.

LEFT: After the collapse of the goalposts Kevin Keelan was taken off the pitch injured.

RIGHT: Norwich City manager, John Bond.

Red Devil's Defeat

The 1974–75 season got off to a great start with Norwich going seven games undefeated. A 2-0 win against Manchester United followed in late September in which Ted MacDougall, one of Bond's signings from his old club Bournemouth (via Manchester United and West Ham), scored a brace. MacDougall rediscovered the scoring boots that had eluded him at West Ham and proceeded to bang in 66 goals in his 138 appearances for City, before leaving for Southampton in 1976. Towards the end of the season the manager felt the need to add something extra and made possibly his best signing for the club when he persuaded Martin Peters to leave White Hart Lane for only £50,000. Peters' influence was immediate and helped Norwich return to Division One at the first attempt, alongside Manchester United and Aston Villa.

Season Stats 1974–75

Ted MacDougall **(42 appearances)**
Colin Suggett **(41 appearances)**
Phil Boyer **(40 appearances)**
Peter Morris **(40 appearances)**
Tony Powell **(40 appearances)**
Duncan Forbes **(39 appearances)**
Dave Stringer **(39 appearances)**
Kevin Keelan **(38 appearances)**
Colin Sullivan **(36 appearances)**
Mel Machin **(24 appearances)**
Geoff Butler **(18 appearances)**
Mick McGuire **(16 appearances)**
John Miller **(14 appearances)**
John Benson **(10 appearances)**
Martin Peters **(10 appearances)**
Billy Steele **(9 appearances)**
Steve Grapes **(8 appearances)**
Roger Hansbury **(4 appearances)**
Doug Livermore **(3 appearances)**
Steve Goodwin **(2 appearances)**

Record: P42 W20 D13 L9 F58 A37 PTS53
Goals: MacDougall 17, Boyer 16, Suggett 6, Machin 3, Miller 3, Powell 2, Stringer 2, McGuire 2, Peters 2, Grapes 2, Forbes 1, Sullivan 1, Butler 1
Manager: John Bond

RIGHT: Action from the 1974 league semi-final. 23rd January 1974, Norwich City 1 Wolverhampton Wanderers 1.

ABOVE: Ted MacDougall on the ball. 28th September 1974, Norwich City 2 Manchester United 0.

LEFT: Ted MacDougall celebrates his second goal.

Ted MacDougall in the air during this League Cup semi-final match, 15th January 1975. Manchester United 2 Norwich 2.

Matchwinning goalscorer Colin Suggett (right) with Ted MacDougall after the return leg, 22nd January 1975. Norwich 1 Manchester United 0.

–LEGENDS–

Tony Powell

Tony Powell was signed for Norwich City from Bournemouth in 1974 in exchange for Trevor Howard, and scored on his debut against Blackpool on 17th August 1974. Powell was known as "Mr Dependable" because he rarely ever made a mistake on the pitch, and was a favourite of the fans, winning Player of the Year in 1979. During his six years at Norwich City he played for Norwich City 273 times, a pretty impressive sum that has only been bettered by 14 men. When he left Norwich in 1981, he moved to the USA to play for the San Jose Earthquakes.

FOOTBALL –STATS–

Tony Powell

Name: Anthony Powell
Born: Bristol, 11th June 1947
Position: Centre-half, Midfielder
Norwich City Playing Career: 1974–81
Club Appearances: 273
Goals: 5

The Name's Bond

Ken Brown and manager John Bond, who played together at Wembley in 1964 for West Ham. Bond took over at Norwich on 27th November 1973.

John Bond with his trademark cigar.

Brown and Bond overseeing training.

City players hard at work.

Norwich City players, who were all former Bournemouth players, with manager John Bond, 21st February 1975. From top to bottom: John Benson, Ted MacDougall, Mel Machin, Phil Boyer, Ken Brown (assistant manager) and Fred Davies (coach).

Suited and Booted

ABOVE: Norwich City FC in London for the League Cup final against Aston Villa, showing off their green suits for their arrival at Wembley.

Norwich were fast building a name for themselves as a cup side, and they reached their third League Cup final on 1st March 1975. Having beaten Bolton, West Bromwich Albion, Sheffield United and Ipswich Town, all after replays, they then faced the might of Division Two rivals Manchester United in the two-legged semi-final. They drew 2-2 at Old Trafford before a Colin Suggett goal saw them squeeze through in the second leg at Carrow Road. As luck would have it their opponents were Aston Villa, now managed by Ron Saunders. The game itself proved to be as much a disappointment as the Spurs final had been, and Villa triumphed 1-0 thanks to a penalty from the usually prolific Ray Graydon.

The Norwich City squad relax at Wembley. From left to right: Dave Stringer, Mick McGuire, Colin Suggett, Billy Steele, Doug Livermore, Kevin Keelan, Phil Boyer, Ted MacDougall, Tony Powell, Peter Morris, Duncan Forbes, Colin Sullivan (Livermore and Steele didn't play on the day).

League Cup Final

John Bond leads City onto the Wembley pitch alongside Villa manager Ron Saunders.

Aston Villa 1 Norwich City 0

THE EMPIRE STADIUM, WEMBLEY
THE FOOTBALL LEAGUE CUP FINAL
SAT., MARCH 1, 1975
TURNSTILES
E
ENTRANCE
84
KICK-OFF 3.30 p.m.
YOU ARE ADVISED TO TAKE UP YOUR POSITION BY 3 p.m.
ROW
31
SEAT
6
CHAIRMAN WEMBLEY STADIUM LTD
NORTH STAND SEAT
£4.00
TO BE RETAINED
SEE PLAN AND CONDITIONS ON BACK

Dave Stringer challenges Villa's Brian Little. 1st March 1975, Aston Villa 1 Norwich City 0.

ABOVE: Duncan Forbes goes for the ball.

LEFT: Here City's Mel Machin palms away a header from Villa's Chris Nicholl and concedes a penalty.

Promotion at Fratton Park

LEFT: Despite City's poor showing at Wembley, they went on to clinch promotion back to Division One after defeating Portsmouth 3-0 on 26th April 1975. Here Mick McGuire celebrates his goal on his knees, flanked by Ted MacDougall and Phil Boyer.

BELOW: Here Martin Peters scores the second goal; the final goal was provided by Phil Boyer.

Duncan Forbes assists Norwich City director Geoffrey Watling with his celebratory champagne.

The three goalscorers Martin Peters, Phil Boyer and Mick McGuire.

1974–75 Norwich City FC team. Back row: Mel Machin, Doug Livermore, Peter Morris, Dave Stringer, Mervyn Cawston, Kevin Keelan, Duncan Forbes, Colin Prophett, John Benson, Colin Sullivan. Front row: Steve Grapes, Colin Suggett, Billy Steele, Trevor Howard, Ted MacDougall, Phil Boyer, John Sissons.

WATNEYS RED

29th November 1975, Liverpool 1 Norwich 3.

Top Flight

The club's return to the top flight saw some major improvements to the facilities at Carrow Road. Seats were controversially installed in the South Stand, money was spent on better floodlights and the club's training facilities at Trowse were upgraded. All was set for an assault on Division One. It proved to be a highly successful season in which Norwich scored 16 victories, enough to see them finish in the top half of the division, in 10th place. Highlights included a 3-1 victory at Anfield, and by the end of the season this seemed an even bigger achievement as Liverpool ended up as champions.

2nd April 1977, Norwich 2 Manchester United 1.

ABOVE:
2nd April 1977, Norwich 2 Manchester United 1. Colin Suggett and Martin Peters win the ball.

LEFT: Hooliganism at Carrow Road, 2nd April 1977. Manchester United supporters attacked Norwich fans at the end of the game and caused extensive damage to the stadium.

ABOVE: The 1978 Norwich City FC team.

Standing: Phil Hoadley, Keith Robson, Jim Fleeting, Martin Chivers, Kevin Keelan, Roger Hansbury, Kevin Bond, Martin Peters, Tony Powell and John Ryan.

Front: Davie Robb, Mick McGuire, Colin Sullivan, Jimmy Neighbour, Graham Paddon and Kevin Reeves.

-LEGENDS-

Martin Peters MBE

Martin Peters is one of the most familiar faces in English football, playing in both the winning 1966 England World Cup squad and the 1970 England World Cup squad. Peters' career started at West Ham when he was just 16 years old, he later went on to play for Tottenham and finally, in March 1975 at the age of 32, his former West Ham team-mate John Bond brought him to Norwich for £50,000. His experience was a huge asset to the recently promoted team in establishing themselves in Division One, and he is arguably one of the Canaries' most influential captures. During his time at Norwich he made more than 200 appearances and won Player of the Year twice.

FOOTBALL -STATS-

Martin Peters MBE

Name: Martin Stanford Peters

Born: Plaistow, 8th November 1943

Position: Midfield

Norwich City Playing Career: 1975–80

Club Appearances: 232

Goals: 50

England Caps: 67

England Goals: 20

Out With the Old

During the summer of 1976 John Bond was active in the transfer market, buying John Ryan from Luton Town and offloading several fringe players, including Peter Morris. In September Bond shocked the whole city when he sold the prolific Ted MacDougall to Southampton for a paltry £50,000. The former Bournemouth striker had scored 28 goals in the previous season and would be sorely missed. Viv Busby from Fulham and Jimmy Neighbour from Spurs were the two replacements, but neither could match MacDougall's goalscoring prowess. Another shock was the sale of club stalwart Dave Stringer to Cambridge United. Kevin Reeves was signed later in the season as Phil Boyer fell victim to an injury and missed much of the second half of the season. And, shortly after his seemingly triumphant return from West Ham, Graham Paddon proceeded to break his leg. Norwich consequently managed to avoid relegation by the skin of their teeth and finished 16th.

The following season proved to be much more successful even though Phil Boyer joined Ted MacDougall at Southampton and Norwich managed only one away win all season. The season was also marred by an injury to Kevin Keelan, who played for most of the match at Bristol City with a broken hand. He missed the rest of the season. The highlights were a 2-1 home win against Liverpool and a 5-4 away defeat at Coventry in which John Ryan missed a last minute penalty. In the end a 13th place finish was highly creditable.

8th April 1978, Birmingham City 2 Norwich 1. Colin Suggett slides in.

26th August 1978, Coventry City 4 Norwich 1. Tough centre-half Phil Hoadley challenges for the ball.

Ups and Downs

As the 1978–79 season got underway, former Spurs striker Martin Chivers was signed from Servette in Switzerland, along with defender Phil Hoadley from Orient, while the ever reliable Colin Suggett left for Newcastle. It was an up-and-down season. Away matches continued to be a problem, with not a single victory recorded all season. The club set a record for the number of draws in a season – 23 in all, including seven in a row at one point. Martin Chivers proved to be a complete let-down and left for Brighton for only £15,000 in February; his last appearance was in a dismal 6-0 defeat at Anfield. Perhaps the brightest moment of the season came when the 18-year-old Justin Fashanu made his debut against West Brom. Norwich ended the season in 16th place, relieved that it had not been worse.

LEFT: Jimmy Neighbour goes up. 28th April 1979, Arsenal 1 Norwich 1.

BELOW: Martin Peters chases the ball.

BELOW: Justin Fashanu against Arsenal's Sammy Nelson

ABOVE & BELOW: Action from the Arsenal v Norwich game which ended in a 1-1 draw.

ABOVE: 18th August 1979, Everton 2 Norwich 4. Kevin Reeves passes to Martin Peters.

The 1979–80 season started with high hopes, and after three matches the Canaries topped the league for the first time in their history. But it wasn't to last and they finished a respectable 12th. It was an odd season in many ways – another one which was full of ups and downs. Kevin Keelan broke Ron Ashman's overall appearance record. Striker Kevin Reeves made his England debut, but was later sold to Manchester City for a club record fee of £1 million. Justin Fashanu was sent off for allegedly kicking an Aston Villa player, provoking uproar in the crowd. Villa goalkeeper Jimmy Rimmer was hit by a coin, which led to a fence being built behind the Barclay End goal. Fashanu then scored what later became the BBC's Goal of the Season in the 5-3 defeat to Liverpool at Carrow Road. And, in another bizarre coincidence, unlikely ever to be repeated, Kevin Bond scored an own goal and penalty in two successive games.

ABOVE: Graham Paddon consoles Justin Fashanu, as he is shown the red card by referee Tony Cox for allegedly kicking an Aston Villa player. 1st December 1979, Norwich 1 Aston Villa 1.

LEFT: Fences go up at the Barclay Stand.

Goal of the Season!

9th February 1980, Norwich 3 Liverpool 5. Justin Fashanu celebrates scoring what was to be the Goal of the Season, a rasping 20-yard volley on the turn.

ABOVE: Martin Peters heads a goal in against Liverpool after only one minute, 9th February 1980.

ABOVE: This is one of the most famous goals in Norwich City history. Justin Fashanu's left foot volley left goalkeeper Ray Clemence clutching at thin air.

BELOW: Fashanu's goal later went on to win the BBC's Goal of the Season, and is still one of *Match of the Day*'s classic football moments.

Fashanu with The Sun Award for his hat-trick in the opening game of the 1980–81 season versus Stoke City.

–LEGENDS–

Justin Fashanu

Justin Fashanu began his football career in 1977 at Norwich City as an apprentice, eventually making his league debut on 13th January 1979 against West Bromwich Albion. His size, strength and power were unmatched by anyone else and he performed wonders at Norwich City. His 1980 goal against Liverpool won him the BBC's Goal of the Season and is still watched by many in awe today. In 1981 he became Britain's first million-pound black footballer when City transferred him to Nottingham Forest. Fashanu went on to play for dozens of teams around the world and was the first prominent openly gay football player; he tragically committed suicide in 1998.

BELOW: Fash enjoys a joke with Kevin Reeves.

FOOTBALL –STATS–

Justin Fashanu

Name: Justinus Soni Fashanu
Born: Hackney, 19th February 1961
Died: Shoreditch, 2nd May 1998
Position: Centre-forward
Norwich City Playing Career: 1979–81
Club Appearances: 103
Goals: 40

Brown is the New Black

Canaries' fans hoped the club's relative success during the 1970s would be exceeded in the 1980s. But the decade got off to a sticky start. Bond had signed the much travelled Joe Royle and then Drazen Muzinic from Hajduk Split for a club record fee of £300,000. After only two wins in their first 10 games, flamboyant manager John Bond departed for Manchester City in mid-October, following a 6-1 hammering at Middlesbrough and a disappointing 1-1 home draw with Wolves. He had been in the post for more than six years, an eternity compared to many of his predecessors, but there had been an increasing number of grumbles from people who felt Bond was getting too big for his boots.

A week later the club announced that Ken Brown would be taking over, with stalwart Mel Machin as his assistant. Supporters were reassured by the news that former players Dave Stringer and Doug Livermore would also be returning to the club in coaching roles. Ken Brown wasted little time in signing Dave Watson from Liverpool, who would go on to win 12 England caps. Soon afterwards Kevin Bond was replaced as captain by long-serving midfielder Graham Paddon. Martin O'Neill was also brought in, along with Arsenal's Steve Walford and young goalkeeper Chris Woods from QPR. Right up to the last day of the season it looked as if Brown had done enough to stave off relegation, but it was not to be. Already-relegated Leicester came to Norwich on the last day of the season and won 3-2. With all the other teams at the bottom winning, Norwich were sent crashing into Division Two again.

ABOVE: New management: Ken Brown (manager), Mel Machin (assistant manager) and Dave Stringer (coach).

LEFT: Sir Arthur South, chairman of Norwich City FC, bids farewell to manager John Bond.

BELOW: The last jackpot tickets to be issued at Carrow Road, 3rd May 1980.

CANARY JACKPOT Nº 20936
SEASON 1979-80
CASH PRIZES:- 1st 50% 2nd 30% 3rd 20%
Cash Prizes allowed under the lottery act
Winners announced at Carrow Road at half-time
(Registered under Small Lotteries and Gaming Act 1963)
THIS TICKET TO BE HANDED IN WHEN CLAIMING PRIZE
ALL CLAIMS MUST BE MADE WITHIN 7 DAYS OF MATCH
NC/WB
Ticket 2p
NORWICH CITY SUPPORTERS ASSOCIATION
Promoter: Ken Marshall
50 KING STREET, NORWICH Tel. 27710
Collectors & Members required for CANARY LOTTERY & BINGO
Apply JACKPOT HUT or 50 KING STREET, NORWICH
F. W. Harrison & Co., (Printers) Norwich

31st January 1981, Leeds United 1 Norwich 0. Tony Powell tries to block a Leeds shot.

Into the Eighties

The 1981–82 season saw a whole host of comings and goings as Ken Brown sought to rebuild the club from top to bottom. Martin O'Neill was sold to Manchester City for £300,000, only to return six months later for £125,000. Justin Fashanu left to join Brian Clough's Nottingham Forest for £1 million and was replaced by Keith Bertschin from Birmingham. Joe Royle was forced to retire through injury so Brown went out and bought the prolific Aston Villa striker John Deehan. Wins were hard to come by, though, and Norwich remained stuck in mid-table throughout most of the season. It was only in mid-March, with the return of Martin O'Neill, that the team started to gel. They went on a 13-game run, losing and drawing only once. It all came down to the last game of the season at Hillsborough. Promotion rivals Leicester City could only draw, so even though the Canaries went down 2-1, it was enough to secure promotion at the first attempt.

ABOVE: Peter Mendham being stretchered off following an injury. 24th January 1981, Manchester City 6 Norwich City 0.

October 1980, Middlesbrough 0 Norwich 1. Steve Goble and Ross Jack are pictured.

31st January 1981, Leeds United 1 Norwich 0. Justin Fashanu in aerial combat, Kevin Bond looking on. Peter Mendham is far right.

LEFT: When Norwich travelled to Hillsborough for the last game of the 1981–82 season they needed just one point to clinch promotion. 15th May 1982, Sheffield Wednesday 2 Norwich 1. Keith Bertschin is pictured scoring the Norwich goal.

BELOW: Keith Bertschin's goal with just four minutes to go sparked scenes of premature celebration from Martin O'Neill, John Deehan and Dave Watson, as Wednesday's Gary Bannister netted a final goal, putting Wednesday in front. Luckily for City Leicester's failure to beat Shrewsbury meant City were promoted anyway.

-LEGENDS-

Dave Watson

Dave Watson joined Norwich City in 1980 from the Liverpool Reserves for £50,000, after being spotted playing at Villa Park in a Reserves game. Watson would help Norwich win promotion in the 1981–82 season and captained City to victory in the Milk Cup final of 1985. During his six years at Norwich he made 256 appearances, and won Player of the Year in 1983. He left City in 1986 to join Everton, earning the Canaries a million-pound profit from the deal.

> *Our jewel in the crown.*
>
> Ken Brown on Dave Watson

FOOTBALL -STATS-

Dave Watson

Name: David Watson
Born: Liverpool, 20th November 1961
Position: Defender
Norwich City Playing Career: 1980–86
Club Appearances: 256
Goals: 15
England Caps: 12

4th February 1984 Dennis Van Wijk and Keith Bertschin challenge for the ball in a 0-0 draw away at Manchester United.

Chris Woods, Age Hareide and Keith Bertschin fend off a Manchester United attack. Mike Channon is the onlooker.

Norwich fans expected a bit of a spending spree in the summer of 1982 but Ken Brown's chequebook was kept firmly in his pocket. The only signing of note was Mick Channon, the much travelled ex-Southampton striker. It came as some relief that the club finished in 14th place. But it appeared the nucleus of a good team was being formed, with Chris Woods, Paul Haylock, Steve Walford, John Deehan, Mark Barham, Dave Watson and Martin O'Neill all playing in more than 35 games.

Martin O'Neill and Steve Walford both left Carrow Road in the summer of 1983 but there were no major new signings. It was a season of mixed results and a 14th place finish was about the best that could be hoped for. Mark Barham was injured in December and was ruled out for more than a year. Perhaps the only highlight was the 6-1 thrashing of Watford in early April.

The 1984–85 pre-season was far busier. A young defender called Steve Bruce was signed from Gillingham, although he didn't endear himself to the Carrow Road faithful by putting through his own net on his debut against Liverpool. But it didn't take long for him to become a Norwich City legend.

Dave Watson observes Chris Woods getting an elbow in the face in the same game.

Fire!

As so often in Norwich City's history, this was a season of ups and downs. One of the biggest disasters in the club's history occurred in the early morning of 25th October 1984, when a massive fire broke out in the main stand. It housed both the boardroom and the team dressing rooms, all of which were destroyed. The stand was damaged beyond repair and had to be demolished.

HEYHOE
RICHIER
FOR HIRE
SHEPHERDS
DEMOLITION LTD
NORWICH
H·48 CK

–LEGENDS–

Chris Woods

Chris Woods played in over half a dozen professional football teams throughout his career, but it was the Canaries where he made most appearances, with 267 in total. At Norwich he established himself as a top-class goalkeeper, playing in the victorious 1985 Milk Cup winning team and helping Norwich to win promotion in 1986. Strangely, he was one of a very small number of footballers to play in a Cup final at Wembley before making his league debut. Woods was always a favourite among the fans, winning Player of the Year in 1984, and was inaugurated into the Norwich City FC Hall of Fame in 2002.

FOOTBALL –STATS–

Chris Woods

Name: Christopher Charles Eric Woods

Born: Swineshead, 14th November 1959

Position: Goalkeeper

Norwich City Playing Career: 1981–86

Club Appearances: 267

Goals: 0

England Caps: 43

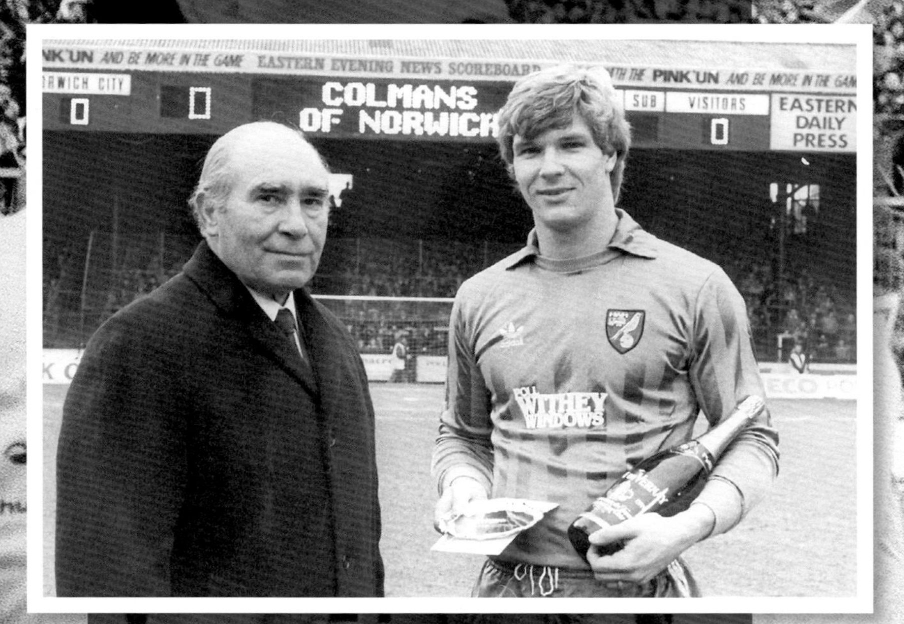

ABOVE: Sir Alf Ramsey with Chris Woods.

Chris Woods with the Milk Cup trophy of 1985.

Preparing for the Milk Cup of 1985.

Norwich's love affair with the League Cup continued in the 1984–85 season, although by then it was known as the Milk Cup. City fans hoped that at long last they would be able to return to Norfolk from Wembley, heads held high, brimming with cup glory. The campaign got off to a promising start with a 6-1 victory over Preston. With further victories against Aldershot, Notts County, Grimsby, and, finally, the Canaries' defeat of local rivals Ipswich Town in the semi-finals, they were off to Wembley.

ABOVE: This is one of the Canaries' most enjoyable moments of the 1980s, Louis Donowa, Mike Channon and John Deehan help Steve Bruce (left) celebrate his goal, which defeated Ipswich and led City to the Wembley final. 6th March 1985, Norwich 2 Ipswich 0.

Cup Glory!

Sunderland were the Canaries' Wembley opponents, so surely this time Norwich could look forward to the match with confidence. Proceedings got off to a rather different, but encouraging, start with an impromptu 60-a-side kickabout outside the stadium between supporters of both sides. As ever with Norwich at Wembley, it proved to be a scrappy, unmemorable match, and when Clive Walker became the first player to miss a penalty in a Wembley final, the Norwich contingent maybe thought that yet again they would return to Norfolk trophyless. But very early in the second half it all changed when Asa Hartford's deflected shot cannoned past the Sunderland goalkeeper. The Norwich end was delirious and cries of 'On the Ball, City' rattled round the old stadium. Norwich held on for the rest of the match and the jubilant scenes at the end of the game are still etched in the memories of those who were there, or who were watching what was Norwich City's first ever live TV game.

Jubilation as John Deehan and Mike Channon realize they have won the Milk Cup.

ABOVE: Clive Walker becomes the first player to miss a penalty in a Wembley final.

"My shot was on target, and although it hit Chisholm on the backside and sneaked in at the near post, when I had finished celebrating I looked up at the scoreboard expecting to see my name in lights. When it was shown as 'Chisholm o.g.', I turned to our manager Ken Brown on the bench and shouted 'Are you going to climb up there and tell them to change it, or shall I?'"

Asa Hartford, the Norwich City midfielder, recalling memories of his winning goal in the 1985 Milk Cup final at Wembley against Sunderland (*Daily Mirror*, 21st May 2011)

Celebration Time

Chris Woods, Dave Watson, Steve Bruce and John Devine celebrate a famous Wembley win in the traditional lap of honour.

Mike Channon hugs triumphant Norwich manager Ken Brown.

ABOVE: The next day the Lord Mayor of Norwich hosted a civil reception and the players toured the city in an open-topped bus, with crowds in excess of 25,000 cheering them on.

LEFT: Chris Woods holds the Milk Cup trophy aloft and celebrates with Dave Watson, Paul Haylock and Steve Bruce.

The Long Road to Europe
1985-1994

Carrow Road restored after the fire.

Relegation

The happiness didn't last. City's league form dived and they managed to win only two of their final 12 league games, inevitably leading to yet another relegation. And to cap their misery, the club's debut in Europe had to wait another seven years due to the Heysel disaster.

Ken Brown was very active in the pre-season transfer market during the summer of 1985, bringing in a whole host of players who would serve the club well over the ensuing seasons. Mike Phelan, David Williams, Kevin Drinkell, Ian Culverhouse and Wayne Biggins would all play a huge part in the club's success in the next few years. Indeed, Kevin Drinkell was the key player in the promotion-winning 1985–86 season, scoring 22 goals in 41 league games. Promotion was secured comparatively early, with a 2-0 win at Bradford City on 12th April, and the club went on to win the Division Two championship. The Yo-Yo had worked its magic again, but this time in an upward direction.

On the pitch, the season got off to a reasonable start and fans started to believe that an immediate return to the top flight was a real possibility. By the end of November Norwich were hovering around the top four and ready to make a push for promotion.

27th April 1985, Everton 1 Norwich 0. Dave Watson and Everton's Graeme Sharp.

ABOVE: Robert Rosario fends off attention from two Everton defenders.

BELOW: Dennis Van Wijk challenges an Everton player.

The Chase

Off the pitch, things were less happy. In early December the entire board resigned over a row relating to the rebuilding of the main stand. Sir Arthur South was replaced as chairman by the ebullient Robert Chase, a man whose natural gift for attracting media headlines was not always well received by the fans in following years. Geoffrey Watling, one of the club's longest serving directors also severed his connections with the board. A new era dawned.

While all this was going on, the team embarked on a 10-match run of victories, including a 6-1 home demolition of Millwall, which saw the Canaries rise to the top of the league – which was where they stayed for the rest of the season. Promotion was clinched with five games to go at Bradford, and the championship was bagged a fortnight later in an away win at Grimsby.

ABOVE: Chairman Robert Chase (right) with vice-chairman Jimmy Jones.

BELOW: 8th March 1986, Wimbledon 2 Norwich 1. Kevin Drinkell congratulates Mark Barham on his goal.

–LEGENDS–

Kevin Drinkell

Kevin Drinkell made his league debut at just 16, for Grimsby, and went on to score over 100 goals for them; Ken Brown spotted his talent and signed him for £90,000 in 1985. He became a hit with the fans for his aerial mastery and opportunistic scoring, which earned him the Barry Butler Memorial Trophy in his first two seasons. He scored 22 goals to secure Norwich promotion to Division One in 1986, winning him the Golden Boot as the division's top scorer. Drinkell is fondly remembered for his goal against Liverpool on 11th April 1987, resulting in a 2-1 victory for City and ending one of the most famous records in football, as it was the first time that Liverpool had lost a league match in which Ian Rush had scored.

FOOTBALL –STATS–

Kevin Drinkell

Name: Kevin Smith Drinkell

Born: Grimsby, 18th June 1960

Position: Centre-forward

Norwich City Playing Career: 1985–88

Club Appearances: 150

Goals: 57

Yo-Yo Club

This proved to be the third time that Norwich had immediately bounced back from relegation from Division One and was to ensure that City became viewed by others as the personification of a "yo-yo club". Following the departure of England players Chris Woods and Dave Watson, many Norwich fans feared what might lie ahead in the 1986–87 campaign, but their fears were misplaced. Some believed the £2 million the club received in transfer fees for the England duo would be used to pay for the new stand and wouldn't be reinvested in players, but Ken Brown was again active in the transfer market and brought in Ian Crook, Shaun Elliott and David Hodgson, while John Deehan went to Ipswich in part exchange for Trevor Putney.

In November, Ian Butterworth was drafted in from Nottingham Forest following a spate of injuries, while Bryan Gunn joined in October from Alex Ferguson's Aberdeen and was to prove one of the club's best ever signings. None of these were exactly star signings, but they gelled in the team, playing some attractive football and racking up the points. Some excellent form around Christmas saw the Canaries climb the league and Kevin Drinkell's steady stream of goals helped ensure a fifth place finish – the club's highest ever in Division One. Had any other player managed to get into double figures, an even higher finish would have been possible. Meanwhile, Steve Bruce cemented his position as one of the league's most impressive defenders.

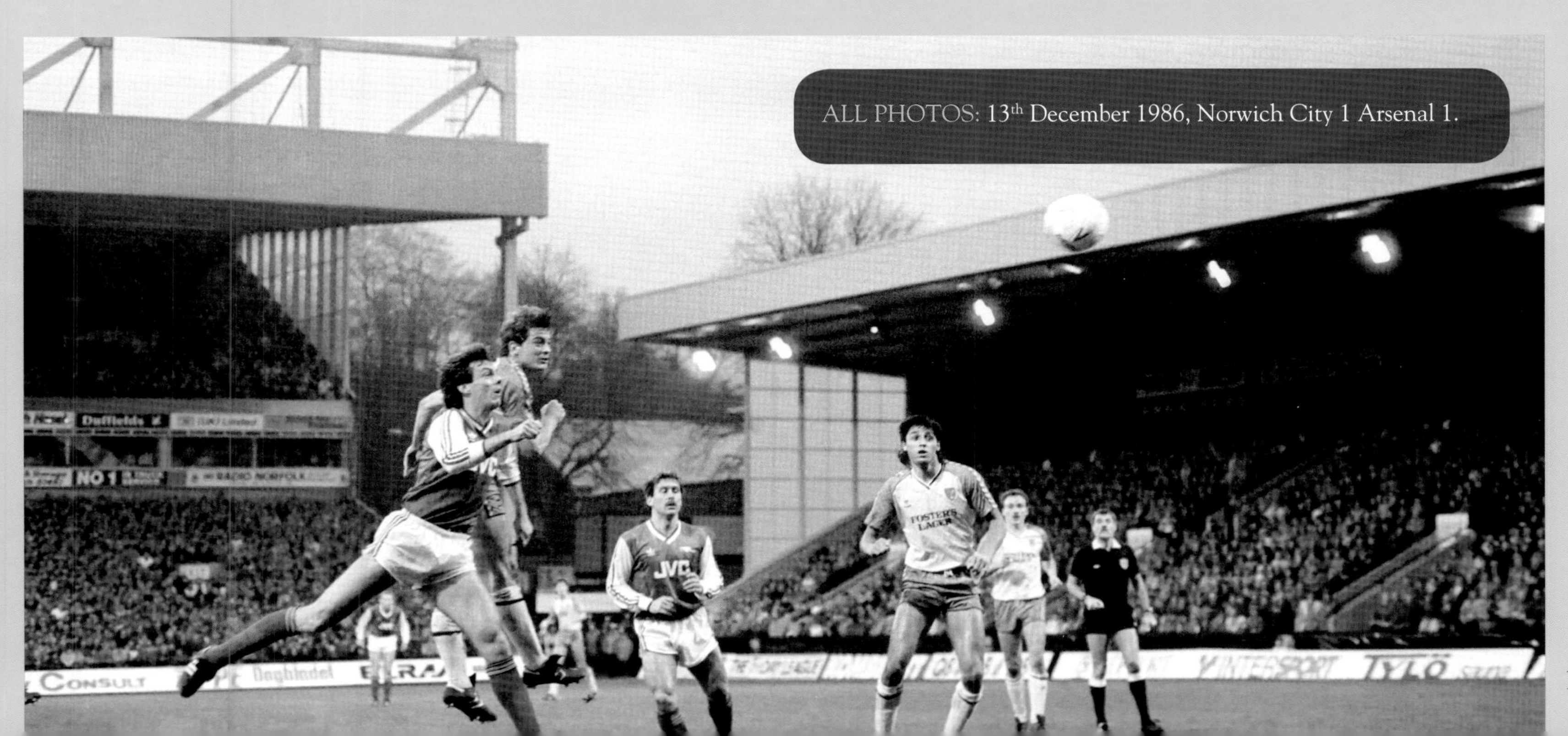

ALL PHOTOS: 13th December 1986, Norwich City 1 Arsenal 1.

Royalty!

As ever with a yo-yo club, one season of success and stability was then followed by the very opposite. Assistant manager Mel Machin had departed to take over the managerial reins at Manchester City, following a path well trodden by Ron Saunders and John Bond. Many blamed this for the appalling start Norwich made to the 1987–88 season, in which Norwich won only three of their first 18 league games. Following the success of the previous season Ken Brown saw little need to change his squad. He didn't even replace long-serving midfielder Peter Mendham, who retired through injury. In early November Norwich lost 2-0 at home to Charlton and it was after this game that the board decided to act, and replace manager Ken Brown.

BELOW: Norwich City FC 1986–87 Team Photo. Back row (left to right): Ken Brown (manager), Ian Culverhouse, Wayne Biggins, Mike Phelan, Robert Rosario, Graham Benstead, Steve Bruce (captain), Shaun Elliott, Kevin Drinkell, Ian Crook and Mel Machin (chief coach). Front row (left to right): Garry Brooke, Mark Barham, Trevor Putney, David Hodgson, Dale Gordon, Tony Spearing, David Williams and Peter Mendham.

Captain Steve Bruce introduces the Duchess of Kent to the Norwich City team during the official opening of the City Stand on 14th February 1987.
From left to right: Bryan Gunn, Andy Townsend, Ian Butterworth, Kevin Drinkell, Mark Barham.

Brown Chased Away

Although the board had decided to let Ken Brown go, it was a pity they didn't see fit to actually tell him. It was only minutes before a hastily arranged press conference that it dawned on him that his departure would be announced at that very press conference. It was no way to treat a man who had brought such success to the club. He appeared close to tears as he recounted his deep love for the club and told local journalists that he was proud of his record.

Mel Machin turned down the opportunity of a return and in the end Chase took the safe option and turned to club stalwart Dave Stringer in what appeared to be an attempt to court popularity with the fans. Stringer endured a very difficult first few weeks, which included the sale of Steve Bruce to Manchester United. But it was the signings of Robert Fleck from Rangers and Andy Linighan from Oldham which helped turn things around. The goals came immediately and Norwich's form over Christmas and into the New Year staved off the threat of relegation, which had looked a certainty only a few weeks before. But again, only Kevin Drinkell got into double figures, although Robert Fleck contributed seven goals in his 18 starts. The club finished 14th, but the Norwich fans would never forgive Robert Chase.

ABOVE: Ken Brown at a press conference about his own sacking.

RIGHT: The new Norwich City manager, Dave Stringer.

–LEGENDS– Robert Fleck

Robert Fleck transferred to Norwich City from Rangers in 1987 for £580,000, and went on to attain hero status among Canaries fans, securing the Barry Butler Memorial Trophy in 1992. Shortly after that he was sold, for the then club record of £2.1 million, to Chelsea. Fleck returned to Norwich in 1995 for the sum of £650,000 and netted a further 25 goals; this brought his grand total to 84 goals in 299 appearances, making him City's fourth greatest goalscorer behind Johnny Gavin, Terry Allcock and Iwan Roberts.

RIGHT: Robert Fleck with team-mate Dale Gordon.

FOOTBALL –STATS–

Robert Fleck

Name: Robert William Fleck

Born: Glasgow, 11th August 1965

Position: Striker

Norwich City Playing Career: 1987–92, 1995–98

Club Appearances: 299

Goals: 84

Scotland Caps: 4

Simply the Best

The pre-season of the 1988–89 season was a time for new manager Dave Stringer to take stock. Goal-scoring machine Kevin Drinkell was one of half a dozen players to leave the club and was replaced by Malcolm Allen from Watford. Andy Townsend also signed for £300,000 from Southampton. The fans looked on in slight disbelief, but they couldn't argue with the fact that Norwich won their first four games and topped the league. And the season just kept getting better and better. Norwich topped the table on 14 occasions and it was only in April that their championship challenge began to fade.

Without a run of three consecutive defeats and a 5-0 away loss to Arsenal, who knows what glories might have awaited. In the end Norwich fans had to be satisfied with fourth place, their highest ever. And, in addition, the club had almost managed to reach an FA Cup final for the first time. The cup run doesn't evoke the same memories as the glories of 1958–59 did, but, nevertheless, Wembley glory seemed within easy reach. To get to the semi-final, Norwich had beaten Port Vale, Sutton United (8-0, with four from Malcolm Allen and three from Robert Fleck) and Sheffield United. They then faced West Ham, who they beat 3-1 after a replay to face Everton at Villa Park in mid-April. Luck wasn't with the Canaries, however, as Robert Fleck was forced to miss the match following the sudden death of his father and the ever reliable Mike Phelan was missing through injury. Everton won with a Pat Nevin goal, but the sorrow of defeat was soon put into context when news filtered through of the tragic events unfolding in Hillsborough.

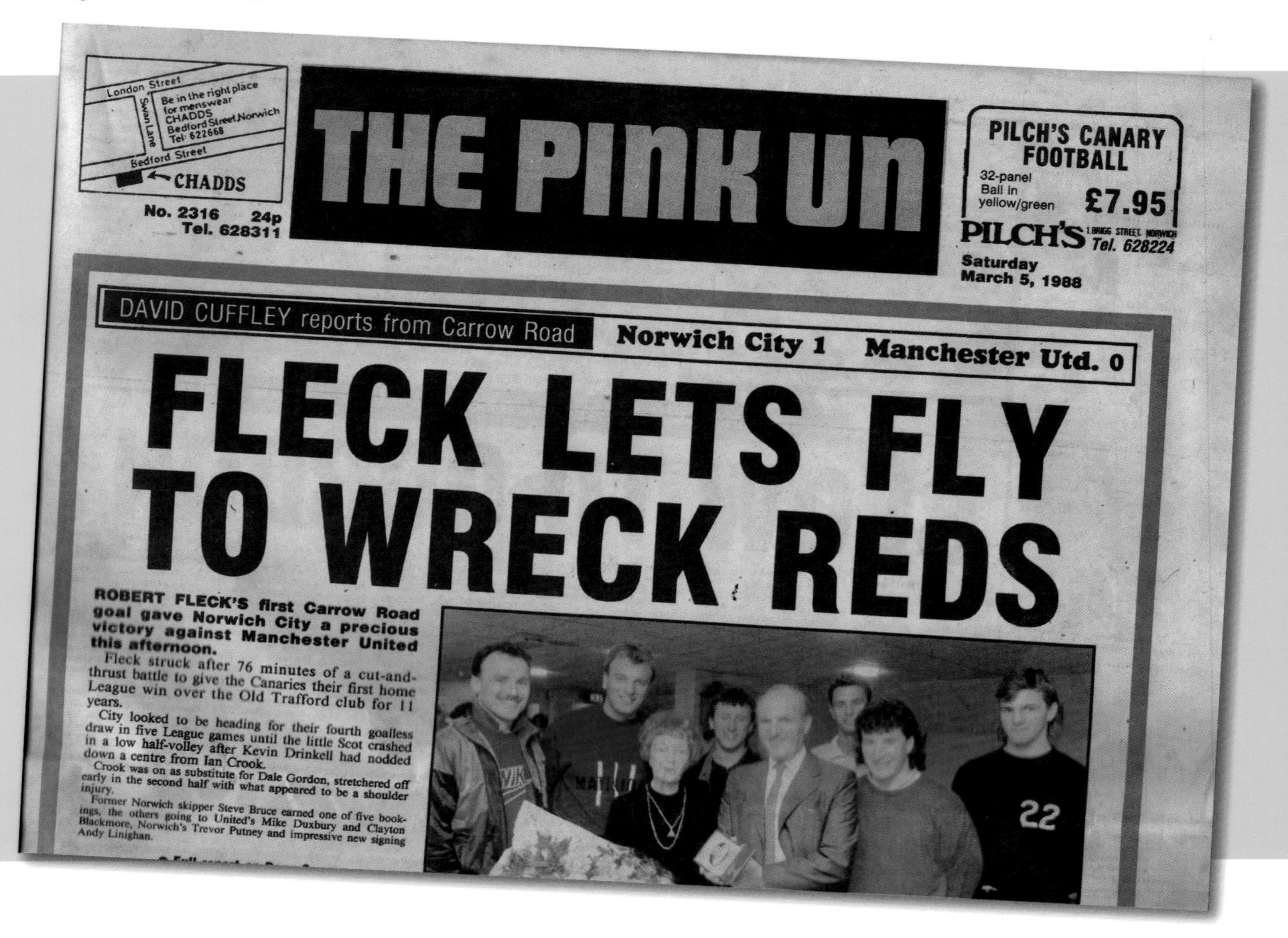

London Street
Swan Lane
Be in the right place for menswear CHADDS Bedford Street Norwich Tel: 622668
Bedford Street
CHADDS

No. 2316 24p
Tel. 628311

THE PINK UN

PILCH'S CANARY FOOTBALL
32-panel Ball in yellow/green £7.95
PILCH'S 1 BRIGG STREET NORWICH Tel. 628224

Saturday
March 5, 1988

DAVID CUFFLEY reports from Carrow Road

Norwich City 1 Manchester Utd. 0

FLECK LETS FLY TO WRECK REDS

ROBERT FLECK'S first Carrow Road goal gave Norwich City a precious victory against Manchester United this afternoon.

Fleck struck after 76 minutes of a cut-and-thrust battle to give the Canaries their first home League win over the Old Trafford club for 11 years.

City looked to be heading for their fourth goalless draw in five League games until the little Scot crashed in a low half-volley after Kevin Drinkell had nodded down a centre from Ian Crook.

Crook was on as substitute for Dale Gordon, stretchered off early in the second half with what appeared to be a shoulder injury.

Former Norwich skipper Steve Bruce earned one of five bookings, the others going to United's Mike Duxbury and Clayton Blackmore, Norwich's Trevor Putney and impressive new signing Andy Linighan.

ABOVE: Tottenham Hotspur footballer Paul Gascoigne argues with City's Ian Culverhouse on the 21st February 1989; the final score was Tottenham Hotspur 2 Norwich 1.

Ian Butterworth of Norwich City chases Frank McAvennie for the ball. 27th March 1989, West Ham 0 Norwich 2.

RIGHT: Liverpool's Steve Staunton tackles Mike Phelan. 1st April 1989, Liverpool 1 Norwich 0.

BELOW: Andy Townsend.

Fight!

The next season was always going to be a bit of an anti-climax, but a 10th place finish in the top flight for a club with limited resources is still an achievement, especially when you continue to sell your best players to bigger clubs. The main departure in the summer of 1989 was Mike Phelan to Manchester United for £750,000, but the club brought in some notable talent too. David Phillips was brought in from Coventry and Tim Sherwood came from Watford. Both would be key players for the club over the next three or four seasons. The season got off to a flying start with Norwich remaining unbeaten in their first nine league games and creating a club record of not letting in a goal in five successive away games.

By Christmas the Canaries had lost only three times – to Luton, Coventry and Arsenal. This was top three form. The only jarring note came in the 4-3 away defeat to Arsenal when a 21-man brawl saw Norwich fined £50,000. As ever, scoring goals remained a stumbling block for Norwich. Only 44 were scored this season. The previous seasons were no better, with hauls of 48 and 40 respectively. The fact that Robert Fleck and Mark Bowen were top scorers with seven, and own goals were the third highest scorer said it all. The next season was even worse with only 41 league goals scored in 1990–91.

ABOVE: A streaker during a match against Queens Park Rangers on 26th August 1989.

RIGHT: Dave Stringer welcomes Tim Sherwood to Carrow Road.

BELOW: A brawl between Norwich players and Arsenal at Highbury on Saturday 4th November 1989. The final score was Arsenal 4 Norwich City 3..

–LEGENDS–

Mark Bowen

Mark Bowen was signed by Norwich City manager Ken Brown in 1987 from Spurs for £90,000. He made his debut on 19th August 1987 against Southampton at Carrow Road, and would go on to make a further 398 appearances for the Canaries. Fans recently voted Bowen the club's best ever left-back and he was also made a member of the Norwich City FC Hall of Fame. In the 1989–90 season he proved he was not just a defender, finishing as the team's joint-top league goalscorer, leading him to win that year's Player of the Year. Bowen still holds the record for the club's most capped player, winning 35 Welsh caps while at Norwich. In 1996 he moved over to West Ham on a free transfer. Mark Bowen will always be remembered for scoring the second goal in City's momentous 2-1 victory away at Bayern Munich in the UEFA Cup in 1994. It prompted John Motson to utter the immortal line: "And Norwich are two up. This is almost fantasy football!"

FOOTBALL –STATS–

Mark Bowen

Name: Mark Rosslyn Bowen
Born: Neath, 7th December 1963
Position: Left-back
Norwich City Playing Career: 1987–96
Club Appearances: 399
Goals: 27
Welsh Caps: 41
Welsh Goals: 3

Mark Bowen celebrates a goal with Andy Linighan and Robert Rosario.

Chase the Chairman

The summer of 1990 saw the two Andys, Townsend and Linighan leaving the club, causing yet more frustration for long-suffering fans who continued to believe the board lacked ambition. Norwich's form in 1990–91 was nothing if not unpredictable. The lowest point was a 6-2 trouncing at home to Nottingham Forest in early January. While relegation never looked a serious threat, a closing run of only two wins in the last 11 games saw the club plummet to a 15th place finish. An FA Cup run to the sixth round was extinguished by Nottingham Forest, but fans remember to this day the fifth-round tie at Carrow Road when Norwich beat a Manchester United team on a run of 16 unbeaten games. Robert Fleck and Dale Gordon scored the goals in a 2-1 win, but it was substitute Ruel Fox who turned the game. Overall, though, Carrow Road wasn't a happy place. Over several seasons people complained the ground lacked atmosphere and the crowd were all too willing to vent their ire at individual players and indeed the chairman, Robert Chase. Chase incurred the wrath of the fans in November 1991 by selling "Disco" Dale Gordon to Glasgow Rangers for £1.2 million. Fans were further annoyed that a player who had never scored more than one goal in a match for Norwich immediately scored two on his debut for his new club. Although Darren Beckford was Gordon's putative replacement, the move didn't really work. Again, City struggled for goals, with only 47 scored in the league. Beckford got seven in 30 games, while Fleck was again leading scorer with 11 in 36.

Chase became even more unpopular among the diehards when it was announced that the Barclay terracing would be replaced by seats, to make the stadium all-seater for the first time. Opponents of the move proceeded to lay a wreath at the side of the pitch and embarked on a sit-down protest during the home match with Arsenal in early April. An unhappy season saw the Canaries finish in 18th, just two places above the relegation zone. But it was nearly a memorable season. When Norwich faced Division Two's Sunderland in the FA Cup semi-final on 5th April, most neutrals expected Norwich to reach their first Wembley final. Home wins over Barnsley, Millwall and Notts County set up a quarter-final with Southampton, and after extra time in a replay Norwich squeezed through 2-1 with a goal from Chris Sutton four minutes from time. The semi-final at Hillsborough was a damp squib. Sunderland scored after half an hour and Norwich just couldn't find the back of the net. Cup glory would have to wait, yet again.

ABOVE: 28th April 1990, Aston Villa 3 Norwich 3. Andy Townsend, Ian Culverhouse and Andy Linigan compete with Villa's Tony Cascarino for the ball.

BELOW: Paul Blades avoids a spectacular overhead kick by Liverpool's John Barnes. 20th October 1990, Norwich 1 Liverpool 1.

A disappointed Norwich City as Sunderland beat them 1-0 on the 5th April 1992, denying Norwich a place in the FA Cup final. Mark Bowen and John Polston are pictured.

ABOVE: Sherwood celebrated his first goal of the match against Sheffield United. 3rd November 1990, Norwich 3 Sheffield United 0.

LEFT: Dale Gordon.

Bring On Walker

During the summer of 1992 Dave Stringer was replaced by reserve team manager Mike Walker. Few could have predicted the instant success he would bring. He appointed former City striker John Deehan as his deputy and sold leading scorer Robert Fleck to Chelsea for £2.1 million, replacing him with Manchester United striker Mark Robins. Indeed, Robins scored two goals on his debut in a 4-2 win at Arsenal. Seven wins and two draws saw Norwich race to the top of the league and even two heavy losses in October away to Blackburn (7-1) and Liverpool (4-1) couldn't shake the Canaries' confidence. It wasn't just the results, it was the style of play and the entertainment Norwich were providing which won them friends all over the country. By December Norwich were sitting pretty, eight points clear of second place Blackburn, but a run of five games without a win knocked the Canaries off their perch.

Form was quickly regained and Norwich remained there or thereabouts for the rest of the season. A real championship challenge was under way. In March Mike Walker sold Darren Beckford and replaced him with the powerful Efan Ekoku. In the end Manchester United raced away with the title and a final day 3-3 draw against Middlesbrough was enough to secure third place, one point ahead of Blackburn and only two behind second placed Aston Villa. It had been a triumphant season for newbie manager Mike Walker and his team. Mark Bowen, David Phillips and Bryan Gunn had been ever-presents. In Gunn's case this was a remarkable achievement as he had tragically lost his baby daughter to leukaemia midway through the season. Goals, for once, had not been hard to come by. Mark Robins top-scored with 15, with Chris Sutton scoring eight and David Phillips nine in a grand total of 61 league goals. And the icing on the cake was that a UEFA Cup place was secured. For the first time, Norwich City would play in Europe. These were exciting times at Carrow Road.

ABOVE: Norwich City manager, Mike Walker.

BELOW: City's Chris Sutton in action at Stamford Bridge. 12th September 1992, Chelsea 2 Norwich 3.

6th March 1993, Queens Park Rangers 3 Norwich 1. Daryl Sutch, Ruel Fox and Chris Sutton are pictured.

LEFT: Ian Crook and Mark Robins high five at Stamford Bridge. 12th September 1992, Chelsea 2 Norwich 3.

RIGHT: Bryan Gunn.

To Europe

The following season was equally memorable. By November Norwich were in third place, but their home form was letting them down. In seven home games the Canaries had only managed to chalk up three goals. But as their UEFA Cup got under way league form started to suffer.

The UEFA Cup campaign began in September with a tie against Dutch side Vitesse Arnhem. A 3-0 home win, with goals from Ekoku, Goss and Polston set up an away leg where they did not concede a goal. For once the Norwich defence held firm in a drab 0-0 draw. It was enough to see Norwich through to the second round and a delicious tie against top German side Bayern Munich. Few could predict what would follow. With the Oktoberfest in full swing, Norwich travelled to the Bavarian capital and after only 13 minutes Jeremy Goss smashed the ball into the net to put Norwich one up.

Seventeen minutes later it got even better for the European debutantes when Mark Bowen popped up to score the second. Bayern got a goal back just before half-time, but again, the Norwich defence proved resolute and the Canaries went into the second leg with a narrow 2-1 lead, with two crucial away goals. The rematch at Carrow Road was a roller-coaster of a game. Bayern scored after only four minutes and the home crowd naturally expected the worst. But again, Jeremy Goss was the hero and his equalizing goal five minutes after half-time ensured he entered legendary status.

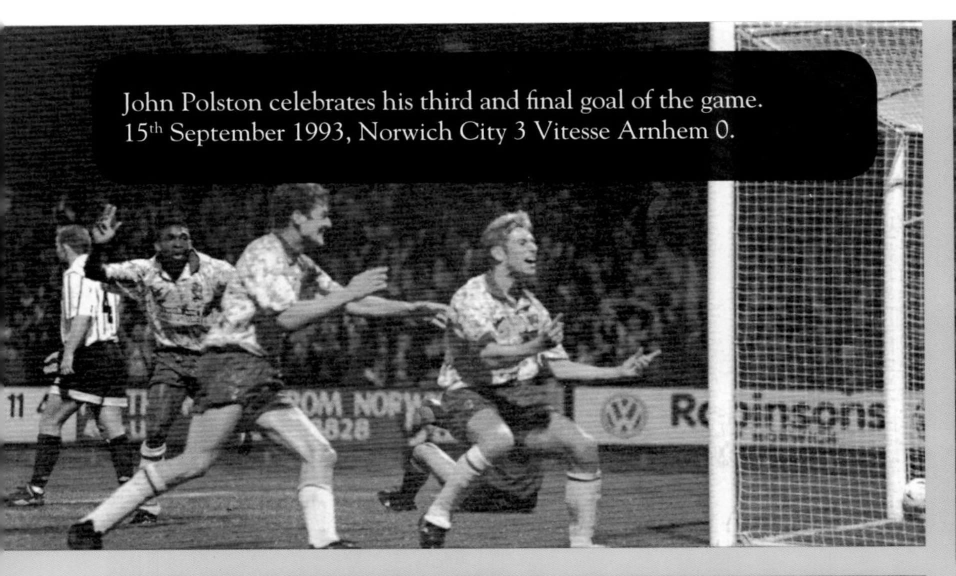

John Polston celebrates his third and final goal of the game. 15th September 1993, Norwich City 3 Vitesse Arnhem 0.

This is quite possibly the most famous image from the 1993 UEFA Cup. Jeremy Goss volleying Norwich into the lead against Bayern Munich in the first leg of the second round. 20th October 1993, Bayern Munich 1 Norwich City 2.

"When he scores goals they're either spectacular or important and that one's both."

John Motson in his BBC TV commentary, Norwich City v Bayern Munich, 3rd November 1993, just after Jeremy Goss had equalized Bayern's opening goal. Goss' goal gave the Canaries a 3-2 aggregate lead.

ABOVE: Goss celebrates his goal during the second match against Bayern Munich, this time at Carrow Road. 3rd November 1993, Norwich City 1 Bayern Munich 1.

LEFT: The Jeremy Goss fan club were out in full force on the 3rd November 1993, during Norwich City's 1-1 draw with Bayern Munich.

"It was disappointing that the Bayern management didn't show us any respect, there was an air of arrogance about them. We used that as a stimulus."

Bryan Gunn

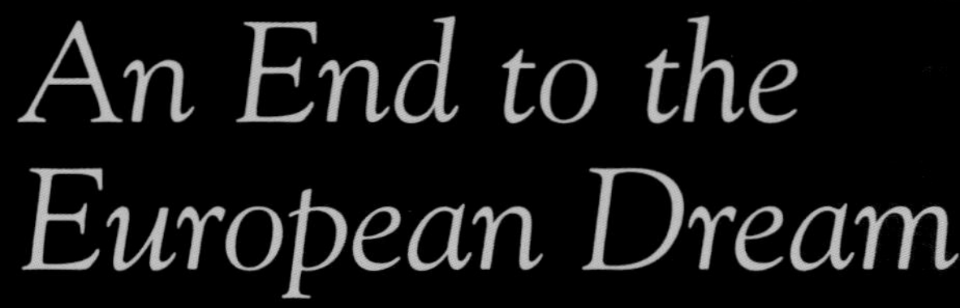

An End to the European Dream

Next up were Inter Milan. Again, the media and the fans expected a drubbing. The teams met in the San Siro in late November and Norwich again showed themselves to be a tight defensive force and it took Inter 80 minutes to break down the Norwich back four with a goal from Dennis Bergkamp. In the return leg it was again Bergkamp who broke Canary hearts, with a very late goal, two minutes from time, doing the damage. The Norfolk European dream was over, but it was a campaign which will long live in the memory of Norwich fans who experienced it.

Ruel Fox kicks the ball. 24th November 1993, Inter Milan 1 Norwich 0.

Rob Newman and Ian Butterworth chase the ball.

LEFT: Lee Power clashes heads with an Inter Milan player.

BELOW: Rob Newman goes in for a tackle.

–LEGENDS–

Jeremy Goss

Jeremy Goss was a member of Norwich City's FA Youth Cup winning team in 1983, and would continue to play for the Canaries until 1996. Goss really came to prominence in the 1990–91 season when he became a regular in the starting line-up and even went on to earn nine Welsh caps. His stunning volleyed goal against Leeds United at Elland Road in the opening month of the 1993–94 season was voted Goal of the Month on *Match of the Day*, and is undoubtedly one of the best goals he ever scored. However, he will be most fondly remembered as scoring one of Norwich City's most spectacular goals against Bayern Munich during the UEFA Cup 1993, which led to Norwich's most famous win, as it was the first time that an English side had ever beaten Bayern at their home ground.

"I didn't have to adjust my stride, I just hit it on the volley with my right foot. It was as sweet as anything."

Jeremy Goss on his famous first goal against Bayern Munich in the 1993 UEFA Cup

Norwich City legend Jeremy Goss at Carrow Road after his winning goal against Bayern Munich in the UEFA Cup.

FOOTBALL –STATS–

Jeremy Goss

Name: Jeremy Goss
Born: Cyprus, 11 May 1965
Position: Midfielder
Norwich City Playing Career: 1983–96
Club Appearances: 238
Goals: 23
Welsh Caps: 9

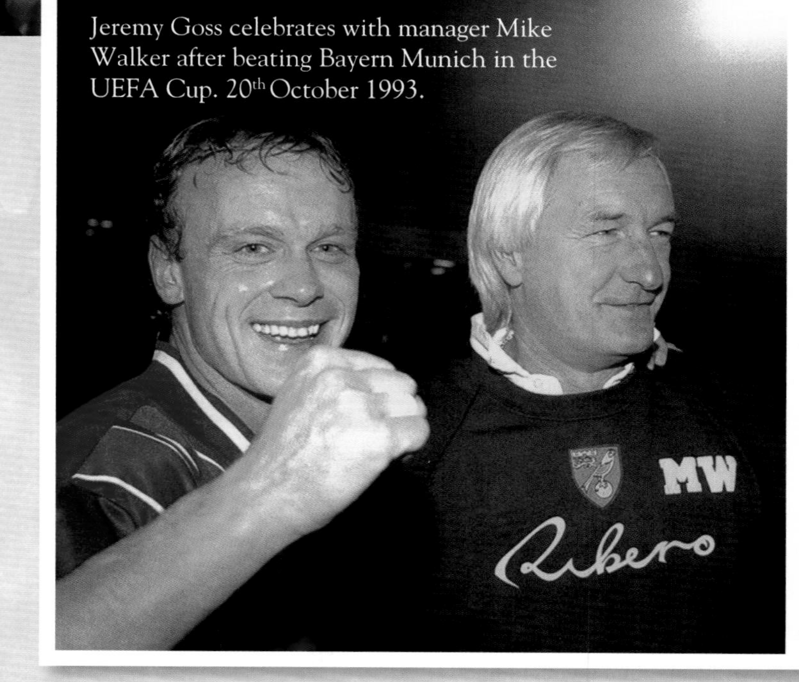

Jeremy Goss celebrates with manager Mike Walker after beating Bayern Munich in the UEFA Cup. 20th October 1993.

Walker Departs

The rest of the season was memorable but for different reasons. Mike Walker had had several run-ins with unpopular chairman Robert Chase not just over investment in the team but also his own terms and conditions. When the Everton manager's position became free, the rumour mill started. An approach from Everton for permission to talk to Walker was rebuffed by Chase, but Walker took matters into his own hands and walked out. The club and its fans were stunned, and some would never forgive Walker for this apparent act of disloyalty. He was quickly replaced by his deputy, John Deehan, who in turn appointed defender Gary Megson as his assistant. Deehan saw how difficult the job would be when star winger Ruel Fox was soon sold under his feet to Newcastle for £2.5 million. It took 10 games for Deehan to register his first win, almost inevitably against Mike Walker's Everton. Things improved for Deehan after that, and Chris Sutton's 25 goals in 41 games ensured he would soon become a transfer target, but a 12th place finish was a disappointment after the triumphs of the previous 18 months.

RIGHT: This photo was taken of Mike Walker three days before his resignation, during the morning of his final match in charge.

BELOW: 30th January 1994, Norwich City 0 Manchester United 2.

LEFT: John Deehan, the new Norwich City manager.

Norwich City FC Player of the Year

1967	Terry Allcock
1968	Hugh Curran
1969	Ken Foggo
1970	Duncan Forbes
1971	Ken Foggo
1972	Dave Stringer
1973	Kevin Keelan
1974	Kevin Keelan
1975	Colin Suggett
1976	Martin Peters
1977	Martin Peters
1978	John Ryan
1979	Tony Powell
1980	Kevin Bond
1981	Joe Royle
1982	Greg Downs
1983	Dave Watson
1984	Chris Woods
1985	Steve Bruce
1986	Kevin Drinkell
1987	Kevin Drinkell
1988	Bryan Gunn
1989	Dale Gordon
1990	Mark Bowen
1991	Ian Culverhouse
1992	Robert Fleck
1993	Bryan Gunn

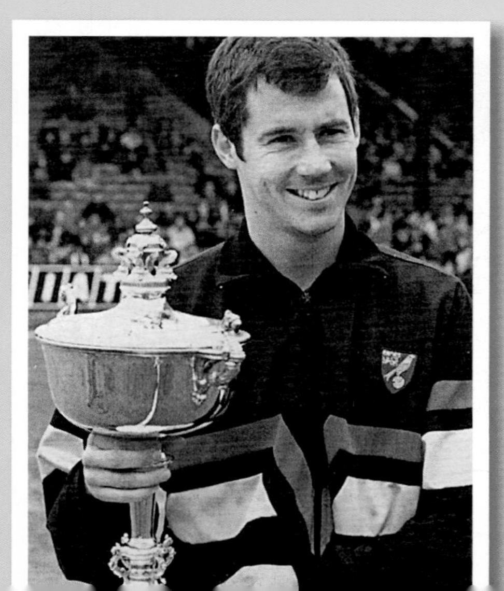

LEFT: Ian Culverhouse, Player of the Year 1991, with the Barry Butler Memorial Trophy.

Martin Peters, Player of the Year 1976 and 1977, with the Barry Butler Memorial Trophy.

Terry Allcock, the first Player of the Year way back in 1967, with the Barry Butler Memorial Trophy.

This book is dedicated to the memory of my aunt, Jean Theobald, who would tootle off up the A11 every other Saturday in the 1960s and 1970s to watch the Canaries. Cancer took her from us in the early 1980s, but her infectious humour remains with me and my family to this day.

My thanks go to MirrorPix Photographic Research – Alex Waters, David Scripps, John Mead, Vito Inglese and Manjit Sandhu.

And to the *Eastern Daily Press* – Pete Waters, Peter Hannam & the EDP Sports Desk. Rosemary Dixon, the EDP archivist and librarian has been a joy and pleasure to work with and has gone way beyond the call of duty in helping us with our research.

To Norfolk & Norwich Millennium County Library for permission to use pictures featured on pages 8, 17, 22 and 27. To Nick Oldham for the caricature of Ron Ashman on page 89 and Jonathan Plunkett for giving permission to use his father George Plunkett's picture of the new Carrow Road ground on page 37.

I'd like to thank Andrew Harrison from the SING UP THE RIVER END! (www.canaryseventyninety.blogspot.com) blog whose painstaking research has been invaluable. I would also like to acknowledge the work of Rob Hadgraft (*Norwich City, the Modern Era 1980-2000*), Mike Davage (*Glorious Canaries Past & Present*), John Eastwood & Mike Davage (*Canary Citizens*), David Cuffley (*The Norwich City Story*) and Ted Bell (*On the Ball City*). Each of their works is an outstanding example of a labour of love and I am grateful to them for the insights they gave me into the club's history and for providing many of the facts and statistics used in this book.

Thanks also to my assistant Grant Tucker who has learned more about Norwich City than he ever thought possible. He now models his hairstyle on Kevin Keelan's.

And to Richard Havers the series editor of When Football Was Football.